Stop It Now or Regret it Later

Stop It Now or Regret it Later

Catharine Ingram

authorHOUSE®

AuthorHouse™ LLC
1663 Liberty Drive
Bloomington, IN 47403
www.authorhouse.com
Phone: 1-800-839-8640

Published by AuthorHouse   02/05/2014

ISBN: 978-1-4918-5919-3 (sc)
ISBN: 978-1-4918-5918-6 (e)

Library of Congress Control Number: 2014901970

Acknowledgment

I want to first of all, thank God for planting the desire to write in me, even when I was in high school. I'm also honored that so many people have been touched in a small way by my "gift." I'm thankful for Thomas, my husband of thirty nine years, our sons and daughter, Michael, Derandal and Michelle, for the support and encouragement they have given me in so many ways while writing this novel.

Chapter One

"Honk." *The sound of a horn blowing.*

"Honk!"

"Hooonnkk!"

In her side mirror she watched as a rusty, old, beat up, red Plymouth pulled alongside of her. The car was shaking and rattling. Rolling his window down, the driver pulled along side of her and sarcastically shouted,

"Stupid lady! What are you waiting on—for the stop sign to change to green?"

With a look of disgust, he snarled, "Women drivers!"

Then he roared off, leaving behind a heavy smell of burnt rubber and smoke. A hanging muffler, tied with a white rag, sent sparks flying as it bounced off the pavement.

Marilyn had refused to make eye contact with the driver since she was very much aware of road rage and its consequences. The local media had recently reported two incidents, each with tragic endings, there had been two incidents reported in the local media within the last month. Both had tragic endings. After checking her rearview mirror she hesitated a moment to put even more space between herself and the irate driver. Alone, she shivered at the thought of running into him again.

It was 12:32 p.m. In fifteen minutes she would be at the correctional facility. Even though she wasn't a highway driver, she had made great time. The forecast prediction of a possible thunderstorm had caused her to consider postponing the trip until the following week. Reggie, however, had begged her to come. Thus, she had reconsidered.

From the moment she got behind the wheel, dark clouds overhead were her constant companions. Yet, six hours later she had not seen a sprinkle of rain. As she pulled into the parking lot, she looked up to see the clearest, most vivid rainbow she had ever seen. It looked like someone had taken a brush and painted it across the sky. A sour, acidic feeling welled up inside her stomach. All her life she had been taught that a rainbow appears at the end of the storm. However, as she turned off the switch she sensed this storm was just about to begin.

The weight on her shoulders became heavier with each step as she walked from the parking lot to the visitors' entrance. It felt as though she were wearing a heavy winter coat. Looking up at the grayish windowless buildings surrounded by yards and yards of barbed razor-sharp wire, only one word came to mind—depressing. As a mom, her worst fear had been getting a call from the school, hearing that her son was injured. Never did she expect to be coming here. Like most moms, she had taught her son not to steal, to avoid gangs, and, most of all, to say no to drugs. Yet, here she was, about to enter one of the loneliest places she had ever visited. Her heart was pounding and her palms were wet as she stepped inside the vestibule.

After having her identification verified she was ushered into a room to be searched. The fact that women executed the search mattered little. Body cavity searches were still the most humiliating ordeal had ever experienced. In order to endure it, you practically needed an out of body experience.

Still shaken from the search, she was sent to the visitors' room. Thirty minutes later Reggie was ushered in. He hesitated as he walked into the room. Seeing her raised hand he smiled as he walked across the floor. Even from a distance she noticed he looked tired, and there were bags under his eyes. A long tiny scar ran down the side of his left eye. It hadn't been there before.

She held her stomach as scenes from old prison movies flooded her mind. She couldn't bear to ask.

She put on a cheerful disposition for him, as she struggled desperately to hold back a floodgate of emotions. He listened attentively, smiling as she related messages from his friends. His face lit up when he asked about the twins. He dropped his head when she told him that every single day they asked about him. They said they wanted their *big brother* to come home.

Marilyn prolonged giving Reggie the bad news for as long as possible. Lately, she noticed his temper had become very short. Any little thing could cause him to blow up. Without coming up for air she ran one sentence right into the next, trying to avoid the inevitable.

Not wanting to hear "I told you so" from her family had forced Marilyn to turn to her friends and co-workers to borrow money. For the third time in as many years, thirteen-year old Reggie had been arrested again. The first two times had been for shoplifting candy in a neighborhood store. Fortunately, after much pleading she had been able to get the store to drop the charges. This time it was more serious. The charge—use of a stolen credit card.

She needed three thousand dollars for a lawyer to even consider an appeal. She had less than three hundred dollars in her savings account. She was unsuccessful in borrowing from her friends. They all cried "broke." Swallowing her pride she relented and asked her aunt and uncle. She'd never known either of them to have financial problems. This time however, they had both given some kind of sad stories about bills. Of course, she didn't buy it. They never tried to hide the fact they thought that Reggie was a spoiled brat who needed some discipline.

Deep in her heart she knew they loved Reggie. Maybe it was because of their age that they had little patience with children. She sensed that they were glad to see him finally get a *reality check*.

After informing Reggie that she was unable to raise the needed funds, she watched as he morphed right before her eyes from a remorseful soft-spoken son to a stark raving stranger. Believing that he would be going home soon, only a few minutes earlier, he had thanked her for being a great mom. He had also apologized, promising to make some positive changes.

With her head down, Marilyn sat stone-faced, listening as her son hurled one accusation after another at her. He accused her of not loving him and wanting to see him punished.

"You don't love me!"

"You don't care if I rot in this filthy place!"

"You're not trying to get me out!"

"What kind of a mom are you?"

One after another he shouted. Each verbal jab pierced her heart as she fought to maintain her composure. Her entire body felt the effect of his rage. Her head throbbed with the worst migraine ever. Her stomach bubbled like peroxide on a fresh cut. Her heart felt like a heavy brick was pinning it down. Her legs were shaking uncontrollably. It took every ounce of her strength to keep her lunch down. She sat and racked her brain trying to remember when her precious little bundle of joy had turned into the spoiled, disrespectful young man that was now sitting in front of her.

He slammed his fist down on the ledge in front of her which caused her to jump.

He shouted, "You don't have to ever come see me again!"

He jumped up, kicked the chair and walked over to the corner of the room.

Marilyn sat numbed. She sat with her eyes closed expecting any minute to wake up from a horrible dream. It wasn't to be. As she slowly rose from the chair her hands shook uncontrollably. As she choked back tears she promised to visit him again soon.

She had to pull herself together. There was a long drive ahead of her. Marilyn closed her eyes and took a couple of slow deep breaths. They were supposed to calm a person down. After two or three minutes, she noticed that, unfortunately, for her they weren't working. She couldn't believe the way her son had reacted. It had to be a bad dream. Never in her wildest imagination would she have believed the way her son treated her today.

She felt disrespected.

She felt violated.

She felt humiliated.

"Slam!" echoed the steel door as it closed behind Marilyn. The impact and vibration caused her to jump. She grabbed her chest as a sharp pain shot through it and caused her to slump to the dirty concrete floor. Ringing out in the corridor were loud shouts from the inmates. They were yelling all kind of accusations.

Some were shouting that they had been framed. Some were asking her to contact their lawyers, calling out names and phone numbers. Some were wolf whistling. But there was one voice that stood out. There was one voice that tugged at her heart. It was the one from her thirteen-year-old son, Reggie.

"Mom, please don't leave me here! Mom, you got to get me out of here! Mmmmooommmmmm, pleaaaasssseeee! I didn't do anything. You never believe me. What kind of mom are you?"

One after another he threw out accusations; each one was like a dagger in her heart.

A gentle hand touched her shoulder. "Miss, are you alright?" the guard asked. He offered his hand. She looked up through tear-stained eyes into one of the kindest faces she had ever seen. Written on it was genuine compassion and concern. Nodding yes, she took his hand as she rose to her feet. The guard saw her lips move. He knew she thanked him, though no sound came from her mouth. She quickly turned and hurried away.

Once outside, she stopped and breathed a deep sigh of relief. There had been a strong rank smell of urine in the corridor that had intensified her migraine headache. Her heart had been pounding the whole time she was in the jail. As she headed to her car she heard someone crying softly. On the bench was a young lady rocking backward and forward. She recognized her as one of the mothers who had been inside with one of the other inmates. She took two steps toward her and stopped.

Her first instinct thought was to go over and comfort her, but she knew that there was nothing she could say or do now to ease the pain. Time would have to heal it.

Nearing her car, she felt for her keys. Her pockets were empty. Dumping everything on the hood of the car, she searched frantically for them. She didn't have a clue as to where she had left them. One thing she knew, and that was she couldn't bear to go back inside, at least not right now. Feeling exhausted she leaned up against the door and rested her head on her arms.

After a few seconds and a few deep breaths, she opened her eyes. Dangling from the ignition were her keys. All the time she thought she had them with her. She had been very careless. However, she now only had relief. After several attempts to start the car, she decided to wait a few minutes, less she flood it.

She locked the door, laid her head back on the seat and closed her eyes. After spending the last few weeks shopping for new school clothes, here she was, the last week in August, visiting her son in jail instead of helping him to make the transition from middle school to junior high. She had been so proud of her son. He had been a big help with the twins even though at times he was rebellious and had gotten in a little trouble in the last few years. What boy his age hadn't? It was understandable; after all, he missed his father.

She turned the key in the ignition. It sounded as though it was going to crank but then died down. After three years she knew what to expect from her old faithful. She'd just have to wait a few more minutes, she concluded, as she laid her head back on the seat rubbing her temple. After a few moments, the headache began to subdue, but the ache in her heart was as strong as ever.

This was the second time she had visited Reggie since he had been convicted and sentenced to eighteen months in jail. She had wanted to visit more often, but the thought of her baby behind bars was just too much for her to take. On one occasion she even drove all the way down but wasn't able to go in. Marilyn couldn't understand where she and her husband, Ben, had gone wrong. Since the day Reggie was born she'd tried to give him everything that he wanted. She often went without things she needed in order to please him. Nothing was too good for her son.

She tried again to crank the car. It sounded like it was going to crank but once again it died out. Tired, sad, lonely and now hungry she glanced at her watch. It was 4:05 p.m. and beginning to get dark. "Lord, please let me get back home this evening," she prayed as she turned the ignition and held the accelerator down to the floor. Immediately the car cranked, purring softly. Relieved she laid her head back on the seat. She took a deep sigh and whispered, "Thank you Jesus! Now Lord, help me get back to Interstate 57." As she pulled the sheet of paper with the directions from under her purse, it tore in half.

7

Chapter Two

Keeping her eyes on the highway, Marilyn pressed the torn pieces together with her right hand. Funny how two pieces of torn paper laying on a car seat reminded her of her marriage. What started out as a beautiful whole had become fragmented. In the early part of their marriage they teased about having to go to the bank together with their canes to cash their Social Security checks in their old age, but shortly after Reggie was born, things began to change.

Looking up from the paper, she noticed that she was nearing her exit, which she missed on her last visit to see Reggie. She had been forced to go several miles before being able to turn around. "Don't want to make that same mistake," she whispered, as she changed lanes. "It should be coming up in about a half mile."

Checking her watch she knew Uncle Robert and Aunt Liz would be worried. She had stayed longer than planned. She'd have to stop and call them. They were a big help after her parents retired and moved to Georgia.

With no children of their own, Reggie had become their pride and joy. Her aunt and uncle often kept Reggie on weekends, showering him with love, toys and trips to the zoo or museum while giving Marilyn and Ben a little time to themselves.

One day after Reggie started talking; he surprised her by saying that Aunt Liz had spanked him on a couple of occasions. Marilyn was furious; after all she didn't spank her own child. By age three, Reggie had gotten to the point where he didn't want to spend the night with them.

Marilyn recalled the first time she had to confront Aunt Liz.

Her opportunity came one Sunday after Aunt Liz invited them to dinner. Ben and Reggie were elated. They thought that Aunt Liz's dinners were the best. Knowing that there was a thin line between Aunt Liz's Sunday dinners and Thanksgiving dinners, Marilyn had insisted on coming early and lending a hand.

"Now, that was a great meal, Aunt Liz," complimented Ben, savoring the last fork full of his lemon meringue pie.

"Go on in the living room; your remote awaits you," Marilyn teased, taking the fork from Ben's hand and the plate from in front of him.

Heading for the door, Uncle Robert nudged Ben as he asked the ladies, "Are you sure you don't want us to do the dishes?"

"Thanks, but we have it," Marilyn replied appreciatively. She didn't notice the teasing in his voice, but Aunt Liz did.

"Well, if you insist," Aunt Liz teased, pulling off her apron.

"Run, don't walk. She's a hard taskmaster," Uncle Robert cried hurrying into the living room.

"I thought you were for real," she heard Ben say before the living room exploded into laughter.

"You don't really know your uncle, do you?" Aunt Liz asked Marilyn.

"I thought he was trying to give us a break since we cooked," Marilyn admitted.

"We are talking about your Uncle Robert. When have you ever seen him with a dish in his hand unless a pork chop or piece of cake was on it?" They both laughed.

"I see what you mean," Marilyn replied.

They laughed and talked while cleaning up the kitchen. With the last dishes dried and put away she knew it was time to confront Aunt Liz. She laid her dishtowel on the counter and turned to her aunt.

"Aunt Liz, Reggie said you spanked him," she blurted out.

Walking into the kitchen Reggie heard the word spank.

"She spanked me these many," he said, holding up two fingers.

"Tell your mama what I spanked you for," Aunt Liz coaxed him.

"I didn't do nothing," he said, dropping his head.

"Reggie, do you remember what happened to Pinocchio?" Aunt Liz quizzed.

Reggie grabbed his nose and ran to his mother. He buried his face in Marilyn's skirt.

"Yes, I had to tighten his little legs up the other day," she confessed.

"And yes, I've had to spank him twice."

"I asked him to stop throwing the ball up in the air in the living room. I politely asked him to go out in the yard and play, and he said you let him play ball in your house."

Aunt Liz waited for Marilyn to deny it; she didn't. Aunt Liz continued.

"I told him that he had to either go outside or put the ball in the toy box. He stomped his foot and said no, and yes I did, I tanned his little behind."

"He's just a baby, Aunt Liz. What do you expect?"

"I expect you to discipline him like your parents did you."

"I don't believe in beating children for every little thing they do."

Aunt Liz looked her straight in the eyes. "Answer one question for me."

"What's that?" asked Marilyn puzzled.

"Have you ever spanked his bottom or his hands?"

Marilyn dropped her head.

"Just as I thought," Aunt Liz murmured shaking her head. "Child, I know you think you are showing love by not spanking him but the truth is, discipline is just as major a part of parenting as feeding and clothing."

Seeing that Aunt Liz was old school she knew that this conversation was going no where. Tactfully Marilyn changed the subject.

Chapter Three

Marilyn checked her watch as she turned onto Interstate 57. She hated night driving. With no cell phone and no knowledge of changing a flat, she was eager to get home before dark. A friend accompanied her the first time she visited Reggie. The visit had left her friend so shaken that Marilyn vowed to make the subsequent trips alone.

Marilyn glanced down at the torn paper on the car seat. She flashbacked to an incident years earlier.

She and Ben had planned to spend the Fourth of July with Uncle Robert and Aunt Liz. During breakfast, she and her husband had a big fight. The argument centered on the proper way to discipline Reggie. Feeling frustrated about Marilyn's defensive attitude, Ben insisted that Marilyn and Reggie go without him. He didn't feel like celebrating and wasn't up to pretending everything was okay.

Marilyn wanted so much for Ben to go. Her pride got in the way of her conveying her feelings, so without a word she and Reggie went alone. It was the first holiday she had spent separated from her parents and she missed them terribly. All of their summer holidays were usually celebrated at Uncle Robert's. He had a screened patio and a large enclosed backyard. The winter holidays were usually celebrated at her parents' home, which included a full remodeled basement with a pool table.

In keeping with the tradition, Ben had packed the trunk the night before with folding chairs, two cases of pop, several large bags of chips, cookies and two rolls of aluminum foil. Marilyn had packed Reggie a set of changing clothes. The beautiful day reminded of the day she and

Ben married. She hoped that Ben would change his mind and come over later. It was only a fifteen-minute drive and she would be more than happy to pick him up.

Marilyn didn't try to make an excuse for Ben. She simply said that he wouldn't make it this time. Uncle Robert and Aunt Liz had exchanged glances. For a while they had been noticing the relationship between Marilyn and Ben. They had tried to talk to her several times about her attitude toward her child. Noticing that she didn't want Ben to discipline Reggie, they suggested that maybe she was being over protective and reminded her that Ben was a kind, gentle father who loved his son.

Aunt Liz had made her blue ribbon seven-up pound cake and her delicious homemade ice cream with chunks of fresh peaches. Uncle Robert had outdone himself on the grill with ribs, chicken and hot links. Mrs. Jones, one of Aunt Liz's good friends and some of the neighbors had brought side dishes. Mrs. Jones also brought their four-year-old grandson to play with Reggie. There were eighteen guests. They had a wonderful celebration.

The weather was sunny but not too hot; the food was delicious; and the company was great. At around six o'clock in the evening with everybody tired, sleepy and stuffed, the Jones were the last of the guest to say good-byes and head home.

After cleaning up the kitchen and putting away the leftovers, Marilyn started tiding up the living room. She put the photo album on the bookshelf.

"I want to see Uncle Bob's pictures. I want to see Uncle Bob's pictures," Reggie chanted jumping up and down.

"Okay, okay," she agreed. She held the picture in front of him.

"See. There is Uncle Bob and Aunt Kate," she pointed.

"I want to hold it," Reggie replied as he snatched the picture out of his mother's hand. He backed up so she couldn't reach him. He pointed out his aunt and uncle.

"Okay, that's enough. We have to put the picture up. It's time for us to go home."

He ignored her.

"Give me that picture, Reggie," Marilyn begged, as she closed the album and laid it on the coffee table.

"No, I want to see it, I want to see it!" yelled Reggie, as he jumped up and down on the sofa and waved the photo.

"Be careful with it, Reggie; don't tear it," Marilyn pleaded.

"I not tear it," he promised, as he pointed them out, insisting on calling them his great grandparents.

"That's Uncle Bob. That's Aunt Kate," he pointed, as he smiled and waited for her to praise him.

"That's right, you are a big boy. You remembered," she said as she reached for the picture. It was a picture of Aunt Liz's parents' wedding day. It was the only one they had been able to salvage after the basement flooded. It was very old and very much treasured.

"I not tear it Mommy," he said, as he fanned it back and forth forward.

"I know, but Mommy has to put it back in the album. You can see it again later," she replied, as she took it out of his hand.

"I want to hold it!" he cried, and stomped. She gave it back to him.

"You can hold it just for a little while," she consented.

The picture slipped from his fingers to the sofa.

He stepped on it as he reached to pick it up.

"Rrrrippp!"

She looked in horror as he stood with a half a picture in his hand and the other part under his foot. Holding up both parts he smiled and said, "Look Mommy, two pictures."

Aunt Liz walked into the room. "Oh no, what have you done!" she shrieked when she saw the torn picture.

"I'm sorry Aunt Liz. It was an accident. Reggie just wanted to hold the picture for a moment."

Aunt Liz's pained expression said it all. Marilyn knew it was her prized possession. It was the only picture that she had of her deceased parents.

Aunt Liz didn't say a word. She looked at Reggie, who, out of fear, had crawled into his mom's lap. She shook her head and walked out of the room.

"It was an accident, Aunt Liz," Marilyn said in a low voice, more for herself than for anyone else. "He just wanted to look at it."

When Aunt Liz returned, she picked up the two pieces of the photo without saying a word. She didn't have to. The look of sadness on her face spoke volumes. Several times she had stressed how delicate the photo was due to age. She had planned to get copies made and the original framed.

"I'm sorry, Aunt Liz. I'll get it fixed." Marilyn apologized, as Aunt Liz walked out of the living room with her head down.

"Reggie, baby you made auntie very sad. I know you didn't mean to, but you did. You are going to have to obey me when I tell you to do something, you hear?" she asked.

"I be a good boy, mommy," he promised, as he climbed onto her lap and hugged her neck.

"If you don't, Mommy is going to have to spank you," she added apologetically.

"I be a good boy, mommy," he promised again as he climbed off her lap. He picked up two of his cars and climbed back on the couch. He lined the cars up and pushed them along the back of the couch.

"Get off the couch with your shoes on, Reggie, and play with your toys on the floor," Marilyn pleaded.

"My shoes ain't dirty," Reggie responded, as he continued to race his cars up and down the back of the couch, stepping on one pillow after another.

Marilyn heard the back door close. It was Uncle Robert. He had remained in the back cleaning the grill and putting the chairs and tables away.

"What's wrong? Why are you crying?" she heard her uncle ask with compassion in his voice.

"What happened to the picture?" she heard Uncle Robert ask. Aunt Liz responded, but it wasn't clear to Marilyn what she said.

"What?" he asked as their conversation lowered to a whisper.

"Sit down, Reggie," Marilyn chided her son.

As though he didn't hear her, he continued to drive the cars up and down the back of the couch. At the end of the couch, he turned and started driving the car up Marilyn's arm.

"Look Mommy. I'm driving on a mountain," he laughed.

"Boy, if you don't stop," she laughed. "I'm going to take those cars and put them up."

"No you ain't!" Reggie retorted.

"Yes, I am."

"You ain't."

"I am, too."

"You ain't, ain't, ain't!"

Feeling bad about the picture and somewhat guilty, she tried to be stern. Grabbing Reggie she sat him down on the floor. "Play with your toys on the floor," she insisted. Sensing that she was upset with him, he sat on the couch beside her.

"I love you Mommy," he said in that sweet way as he gave her a big hug. She knew he was trying to keep from getting a spanking. She softened as he planted kisses all over her face. She knew that she should spank him, but she didn't have the heart. After all, it was an accident.

Uncle Robert came into the living room and sat across from Marilyn and Reggie. He didn't say a word, but his facial expression said a lot. After a few minutes he reached down and picked up the remote control. He turned the television off and laid the remote down.

"We have to talk, Baby Girl," he said with a serious tone.

"I want to watch that!" Reggie shouted the moment the T.V. went black.

As Marilyn and Uncle Robert looked on, he reached for the remote control. Uncle Robert was quicker. He grabbed it first.

"Mommy, I want to watch television," he whined.

"*Reggie, go in the kitchen while I talk to your mom,*" *Uncle Robert insisted.*

Without taking his eyes off his uncle, Reggie slid closer to Marilyn. "Go in the kitchen with auntie, baby; I'll be there in a minute," Marilyn said nudging him. Reggie didn't move.

"*Go in the kitchen with your auntie," Uncle Robert said in a stern voice. He pulled a ruler off the top of the bookshelf. Reggie recognized it. It was the one Aunt Liz had used to spank him. He snuggled closer to his mom.*

"*Go into the kitchen now, young man," Uncle Robert said, as he raised his voice as he stood to his feet. Uncle Robert stood six feet four inches tall and weighed over two hundred and fifty pounds; he was a big man.*

Reggie looked to his mom for support. Her head was down.

"*Did you hear me?" his uncle bellowed.*

Reggie looked to his mom for support again. Getting none, he reluctantly walked out of the room.

Alone, the two of them sat silently for a moment. It was an awkward moment. There had never been tension between the two of them. She could talk to Uncle Robert when she couldn't talk to her father. Her father was the serious one of the two brothers. Uncle Robert always had jokes or stories about the war, but not today. Today there were deep frowns across his forehead and his jaws were clenched. His head hung down. He sporadically flinched his jaws and fidgeted with his hands.

"*We keep telling you the same thing, Baby Girl. When are you going to listen?" he asked, with a look of concern etched across his face.*

"*I am truly sorry about the picture, but it was an accident. It could have happened to anyone," she pleaded.*

Uncle Robert shook his head in disbelief. He got up and walked over to the window. As he peered out he searched for the right words to say. It was obvious that she was in denial. However, he was not going to sit silently and let it happen.

"You just don't get it, do you?" He turned and looked at her sadly.

"It's not about the picture. It's not about the broken lamp. It's not about him hitting you back. It's not about ANY one thing. It's about him not listening to you when you tell him something. It's about him wanting to have his own way all the time."

He racked his brain trying to remember one of the worst-case scenarios.

"What about Reggie's birthday party? You were sitting at the table when Ben told Reggie to put the pop back in the fridge. Instead of putting it back, he turned to you like his father hadn't said anything. Instead of you agreeing with your husband, you gave Reggie permission. How do you think that must have made Ben feel? And if that wasn't bad enough you did it in front of his friends, Dave and Kelvin."

Looking annoyed that her uncle was accusing her of treating her husband unfairly she asked, "Is that what he said?"

"No. You know that he's not the kind of guy to talk behind your back." He hesitated. "When your parents moved, Liz made me promise that I wouldn't be a meddling uncle. But that night when I saw the look on Ben's face . . ."

"Reggie is just a baby," she said defensively.

"I'm not going to beat on my child for every little thing he does. I know it's hard for you and Aunt Liz to understand raising a three-year-old since you don't have children. You can't compare today with when you were a child. Times are different now."

"He's not a baby! He's a growing boy who plays you like a fiddle." (He hadn't meant to go there. It was too late to turn back now. Besides, he didn't want to.)

"What about last weekend? The incident with the dollar?" Marilyn looked puzzled.

"Remember, you were going to PAY him to go to bed!"

Remembering, she tried to brush it off.

"Ah, that," Marilyn responded.

"Yes, that! After asking him to turn off the television and take his bath TWICE, you were going to reward him by giving him a dollar?" He asked in disbelief. He didn't wait to hear her answer. He continued, "Maybe he didn't hear you the first time. But when he gave you that innocent little smile it would have immediately been turned upside down. I would have spanked his little behind."

"Spanking is not always the answer," she said in her defense.

"I agree, spanking is not the answer to every problem," he concurred. He was tempted to add, "It sure is the answer to this problem." But he held his tongue.

Uncle Robert knew that the conversation wasn't going anywhere. He'd tried to reason with her so many times before. She just had a closed mind when it came to her child. He knew there was a strong bond between Marilyn and Reggie. Nonetheless, it grieved him tremendously that she could not see that she that her son needed discipline.

He turned and looked at her with love and compassion. He knew she just wasn't getting it. Scratching his head he walked over to the couch. He sat next to her.

"Baby Girl. You, Ben, and Reggie are my family. More than anything I want you all to have a great life. There's nothing that I wouldn't do

to help you. I'm going to tell you what my dad told me. Either you get them in line when they are little, or the police gonna do it for you later."

"Don't start wishing no bad stuff on my son. He's just a kid!" she snapped back. She was getting annoyed at other people telling her how to raise her child. This was the second time this week that someone had tried to tell her how to raise her son. She didn't appreciate her neighbor saying it, and it wasn't going over well coming from her flesh and blood.

Embarrassed at the way she yelled at him, she softened her words. Grabbing both of his hands and looking him straight in the eyes, she smiled. "We love you also. I know you mean well but we are going to be fine. Believe me, all kids go through that talking back and not obeying stage."

"You have to start . . . ."

She cut him off. "We are going to be fine." He recognized the tone of her voice. It said that the discussion was over. He gave her a hug and stood up.

Oddly, he remembered his father words: "You can lead them to the water but you sho' can't make them drink."

Feeling the tension in the air Marilyn grabbed her purse and picked up Reggie's toy cars. "It's getting late. We have to be going."

Like always she gave her uncle a big good-bye hug. Somehow he sensed this one was different. There was tension. She thanked him for always being there for her and her son, assuring him again that everything was going to be fine.

With his arm around her shoulder they both walked into the kitchen. Aunt Liz and Reggie were sitting at the kitchen table drinking milk and eating peanut butter cookies.

Reggie spoke first. "Look Mommy. I got two cookies."

"Mmm! Those look good. Can I have one?" she asked playfully.

"No, these are mine!" he yelled. He quickly hid them behind his back.

Marilyn tried not to show her embarrassment.

"It's time for us to go. Tell Aunt Liz and Uncle Robert thank you for inviting us over," she urged Reggie.

"Thank you for inviting us over," he repeated.

"You are certainly welcome," Aunt Liz bowed. Reggie turned to his uncle. "Thank you, Uncle Robert."

Uncle Robert nodded, "See you later, son. Be a good boy."

Aunt Liz walked them to the car, while Uncle Robert placed the empty glasses in the sink. After he raked cookie crumbs from the table with his hand, he bent down and picked up a cookie from under the side of the table. He dropped it in the garbage and dusted his hands. His spirit was grieved.

Marilyn had left her keys on the cocktail table. As she walked back into the living room she overheard Uncle Robert talking in the kitchen. She listened.

"When is that child going to come to her senses? Doesn't she see that she's not helping that boy? That boy's so rotten he s-t-i-n-k-s. Lord, help her to see that either she must stop it now or regret it later."

He took the newspaper off the top of the refrigerator and laid it on the table. Pulling his glasses from his pocket he sat down and read across the front page in bold print:

School Curriculum Revised

"Well, it's about time. Something is wrong when a school system prepares young girls and boys for practically every situation in life

except the one they most likely will need. I understand why they teach them how to fix a car, how to sew a dress, make a meal, how to drive, and how to cook. But for the life of me I still haven't figured out why you need to know how to do geometry, dissect a frog or speak a foreign language."

He shook his head. "What they need to do first is teach these young folks how to say "no" to their children before they teach them how to say "no" in three new languages."

Folding his paper he continued: "Spanish is fine, but the closest some of them is going to get to anything Spanish is Taco Bell; but all of them will be involved, in some form or fashion, in raising a child."

He shook his head again, as he turned off the lights. "Sure glad Lizzie didn't hear me. She'd call me crazy if she heard me in here talking to myself."

Marilyn, quietly, walked back out the front door. She never said anything to Uncle Robert about what she had overheard.

Chapter Four

Marilyn pulled into the service station to call Uncle Robert. Noticing her gas gauge registered half full, she parked away from the pumps. It was more than enough to make it home. She fished quarters from her purse for the pay phone.

Uncle Robert answered the phone. He assured her that the twins were fine. Aunt Liz had fallen asleep while reading them a bedtime story. After learning that Reggie was fine and that she was going to be late, Uncle Robert volunteered to keep the twins for the weekend. No need to interrupt their sleep. He teased her, saying that since she had lost weight, she couldn't possibly carry two sleepy five-year olds. That was about eighty pounds of dead weight. They would see her Labor Day.

Marilyn gave the attendant a twenty. She paid for the gas and purchased some candy bars for the twins. They always expected something when she returned from her trips. As he counted out her change, she asked if he could check her tires.

"I can't leave the register, but I can get you some help."

"Thanks," she replied walking out the door. The attendant knocked on the window to get another young man's attention. He pointed toward Marilyn as she got in the car.

"I just need my tires checked, please," she said as he walked toward her.

"Yes, Ma'am," he replied, as he walked around the car he kicked each tire.

"Your tires are fine Ma'am." She offered him a dollar.

Refusing it, he waved his hand, "No, Ma'am, it was nothing."

He waved as she pulled out of the parking lot. Huh, a nice touch of Southern hospitality in Illinois, she thought. She smiled.

Taking the north ramp toward the interstate Marilyn picked up speed as the lane began to merge. She became aware of a knocking coming from the car. Panic began to set in. She was over 110 miles from home, with no cell phone and no knowledge about cars. She didn't even know how to change a flat.

One thing she did know, though, was that a car's trouble could be compounded if one continued to drive while neglecting the problem. With less than a hundred dollars in her purse, she couldn't afford to take chances. She pulled to the shoulder.

Without a clue as to the cause of knocking, she did the only thing she knew to do. She popped the hood. Nothing seemed out of order. There was nothing hanging or unattached. She closed the hood and walked down the driver's side of the car to the rear. She checked the muffler. It looked okay.

The sun was setting. It would be getting dark soon. As far as the eyes could see, there was not a single sign of life. There was not even a distant farm. Her heart began to pound. She found comfort in the fact that she was on a major interstate. Hopefully, it would be just a matter of time before a road service truck came along.

She climbed into the car and reached for one of the candy bars. Right now, she needed some comfort food.

Putt. Putt. Putt.

A vehicle had pulled behind her. Someone was finally coming. It wasn't a road service truck, and it wasn't a highway patrolman, but desperation wouldn't allow her the luxury of being fearful.

She watched the stranger in her rearview mirror as he approached her car.

"What's the matter? Did it just stop on you? You're not out of gas are you?" the driver asked, as he wiped his brow.

As she noticed the car grease on his hands, he looked like a mechanic, Marilyn's spirit increased when she observed what appeared to be automobile oil on his hands.

"No, it didn't stop but I heard a knocking, and I was afraid that if I kept driving it would make the problem worse."

"Turn the key," he said. He listened for a moment. Puzzled, he scratched his head and instructed her, "Turn it off and pop the hood," as he walked to the front of the car.

She watched as he shook one thing after another. He closed the hood he got down on his knees and examined underneath the car. He dusted off his pants, scratched his head, and walked to the rear of the car. He checked the muffler and walked around to the passenger side. He smiled and beckoned for her.

"I see your problem."

She walked to the back of the car and there hanging was her gas cap. She had forgotten to close it.

He smiled, "I'm sure glad it wasn't anything serious. I've had enough work for one day with my old heap. By the way, my name is Steve. Would shake your hand but," he held up his hands to reveal dirt and grease, then he headed toward his car.

"Wait." She took a ten-dollar bill from under her floor mat.

"I really appreciate your help. It's the least I can do," she added, as she offered it to him.

"Aw shucks, it was nothing," he replied waving his hand.

"Besides with my old car I might need a helping hand before I get back to Arkansas. Didn't want to put it on the road, but had to go see my daughter. She done messed 'round and got herself locked up. She looks okay."

Shaking his head he continued, "I'm just coming back from seeing her. I have to pick up her stuff in Rockford then I'll be heading home. This has got to be the most trying week of my life. I was having such a pity party. I started to pass you up, but I couldn't."

For the first time she noticed his eyes as he stared down the highway in the direction from which he came. There was sadness that only another broken-hearted parent could perceive.

"It's not much, but, please, just in case." Marilyn insisted, as she held out the bill.

"Can't, Ma'am. Only thing I need is a pump with cold, clear fresh running water."

Marilyn signaled for him to wait. She pulled her keys from the ignition and walked back to the trunk. She raised the trunk hood and opened a cooler filled with bottles of water.

"It's not a pump, but it is fresh, cold and crystal clear," she tossed one then two bottles in the air.

"Thanks," he replied. He caught them one at a time. He rubbed a bottle across his forehead. He twisted the cap, turned the bottle up, and brought it down only after he had emptied it. He threw the other bottle into the backseat, and opened the car door.

With one foot in the car he called out as she got in her car, "I'll trail you for a few minutes. Make sure you are okay."

"Thanks again," she yelled, as she pulled onto the interstate.

Looking in her review mirror she smiled as he pulled onto the interstate behind her. So many kind people had touched her life. Sure there had been a lot of sad days and lonely nights since Ben left, but something always happened to encourage her, to make her smile.

After trailing her for over a mile, he passed her. She waved. He honked and left a cloud of smoke and the smell of burnt rubber.

Marilyn looked in amazement as she observed the hanging muffler tied with a white rag. The irate driver had not been some short-fused weirdo to be feared, but rather a distraught father with an aching heart.

Chapter Five

Stepping up to the desk, Ben smiled politely. As he took out his wallet, he made his request. "Ticket for one. Coach. Chicago, please."

"Will that be window or aisle, sir?" the attendant asked typing in his information.

She looked up and noticed his hesitation. There were so many thoughts running across his mind, he knew that a window with a view would be a waste on him.

"It doesn't matter."

He checked his watch. It was 8:08 p.m. In less than six hours he would be in Chicago. His stomach began to bubble. He wasn't sure whether it was from the butter pecan ice cream or the fear of returning home. It had been six years since he had packed his bag. He had left his wife and seven-year-old son with only a note.

Marilyn turned at 119th and Western. A peace came over her as she parked in front of her building. She turned off the ignition and thanked God for a safe trip. As she grabbed here purse, she noticed the time. It was 10:08 p.m. She was about to close the door when she remembered her keys. She took them out of the ignition and saw the candy bars lying on the front seat. She quickly scooped them up and closed the door.

As Marilyn walked into the vestibule, she pulled her mail from the box. Among the sale fliers and preapproved credit card applications was Ben's monthly envelope. She ripped the junk mail and dropped the envelope in the side of her purse.

"No place like home," Marilyn muttered unlocking the door.

"Aacchoo!"

Marilyn twitched her nose and pulled a tissue from her purse. She pulled a partially sucked mint from the tissue and dabbed the mucus from the tip of her nose. The long trip and broad range of emotions had sapped her energy. To reduce the risk of falling asleep, she had turned the air conditioner in the car on high. Her sniffles were unintended consequences of exercising precautions.

The apartment was dark. She flipped the light switch as she closed the door. Her keys fell to the floor. Exhausted, she waved her hand as if to say, "Oh well." She kicked her shoes off and pushed them in the corner.

Marilyn slung her purse in the chair and dropped down on the couch. She held the envelope up to the light. There was no letter, just a money order.

She mused that her aching body could benefit from a bath with Epsom salt.

In the past, whenever she came home from work, Ben would fill the tub full of warm water and dump a half of a box of Epsom salt.

Six years had passed since Ben had left, but she missed him just as much as ever. Marilyn stretched her legs across the coffee table and rotated her shoulder to get the stiffness out. She then picked up her book and counted the unread pages. Eleven.

This was her favorite time of the day. The ticking of the dining-room clock was the only sound in the house. The house was so quiet you could hear the clock in the dining room ticking. She loved her children, but every mother needs time for herself.

She missed Ben. Things had been so different before he left. She never worried about the bills, laundry or gas in the car. Benjamin had taken care of those things.

"No need of complaining," she murmured as she stretched her left leg at the beginning of a Charlie horse. She closed the book and laid it on the edge of the table. It fell to the floor. She extended her arm, but was unable to reach it.

Turning over she decided to rest a few minutes before going to bed. She turned over on the couch but knew that she would have to soon go to bed. She twisted and turned before she found a comfortable position. She picked up the photo on the end table. It was a picture of her and Ben. It had been taken on their second date. Ben had paid a kid, who had playing on the monkey bars, fifty cents to take it. The child was only about nine.

They wondered whether or not he had taken pictures of their heads. Surprisingly, the photo captured the beauty of their relationship. She wiped fingerprints off the picture and placed it back on the table. She smiled and recalled the first time she laid eyes on Ben.

It had been late one Friday evening after a long and tiresome week. With no food in the fridge and no energy to cook, she had decided to stop at the grocer to pick up some milk, fruit and veggies for the weekend. She had expected to have a simple weekend, not requiring a stove or pot. Everything she had planned to eat would either be taken from a carton, a bag, a peel or a shell.

The trip to the store got off to a bad start. First, there was not one shopping cart in the store. While she stood and contemplated whether she could go back outside to retrieve a cart from the parking lot or carry the few items in her hand, someone spoke.

"Miss, you can have my cart."

She turned to see a tall handsome young man in his early twenties pushing a cart and smiling as he walked toward her. He pushed it up to where she was standing and bowed.

"Ah, thanks. That's nice of you," she replied gratefully and with relief.

She reached for the cart but noticed that he continued to hold the cart.

"My name is William. What's yours?"

Okay, I see where this is going, she thought. Since when do you have to have a formal introduction to give someone a cart?

Pushing it gently toward him, she said, "On second thought, I don't need one. Thanks."

She was miffed to think that what she had thought was an act of chivalry had been nothing but a selfish ploy to engage her in conversation. As she turned on her heels she heard him call out, "stuck-up." She walked on without looking back.

The store had been remodeled, and the milk was no longer in the same aisle as the cheese and butter. The stock boy directed her to the far right at the back of the store. As she picked up the carton of milk, she glanced down the aisle. The Good Samaritan was standing in the same spot with his cart looking out of the entrance door. She smiled.

"I guess he's waiting for the next young lady in distress." She mused and shook her head in disbelief.

As she cradled the carton in her arm she noticed that she had picked up the wrong milk. She placed the carton back on the shelf and replaced it with two percent.

She couldn't wait to get home and get out of her heels. In the future she would keep gym shoes in her car for days like these.

Marilyn made her way to the produce; she needed fresh vegetable. She chose some tomatoes, cucumbers and a head of lettuce to make a salad. In the fruit aisle, as she examined some nectarines and peaches she sensed that she was being watched. Out of the corner of her eye she saw a tall man in his early twenties looking in her direction. He was holding two cantaloupes.

Here we go again, she thought to herself. I guess the supermarket must be the new pick-up spot. Well, I got news for you my brother. Smiling, she whispered under her breath, "Come on, shoot your best shot." Tired from an exhausting day, fatigued, hungry, upset about not having a cart and having to carry her groceries in her arms, she was about to give this brother a run for his money.

"Miss, can I ask you for a favor?

Her eyebrows shot up. She wasn't in the mood for this again. She started to walk away, and then stopped. It's time to nip this in the bud once and for all. There was so much she wanted to just blurt out, but she kept her cool.

"I'm listening," she replied with a smirk. Her tone said, "I'm ready for your line brother. Come on with it."

He perceived her cynical attitude and changed his mind.

"Sorry, that's okay. Honestly I didn't mean to bother you," he tried to assure her and started to walk away.

"No, you stopped me." She was not willing to let him off the hook that easily. "Go on, what's the favor?"

Usually she would just smile and keep walking when guys would throw out their pick-up lines. They'd say stuff like "God must have thrown away the mold when He made you," or "Your name must be candy, 'cause you sure do look sweet". The lines had been around for centuries. They never said anything original.

"Well it's just that I noticed . . ."

"I noticed that you are such a . . . such a beautiful young lady," she said, finishing his sentence and throwing her arms in the air. "Right, I mean, that was what you were getting ready to say?" she asked accusingly.

She thought. I knew it, the same old line. If I had a dollar for every time I heard it, I could buy a brand new car and pay cash for it.

"No, that's not what I was going to say," *he replied and looked puzzled.* "I mean you are, but that's not what I was going to say."

Her face felt flushed. It was not from the compliment but from the smirk on his face. She wondered what he must have thought of her. Was she conceited or paranoid?

"Every time I pick fruit it looks pretty, but it's not sweet. I noticed how you pick your fruit. You seem to know what you are doing. I was wondering would you pick a cantaloupe for me, please."

She noticed that he asked in a way that said that's all I want.

Embarrassed, she extended her hand. She didn't want him to leave thinking that she was some deranged person. He hesitated, took it and forced a weak smile.

"I'm Marilyn McNeal. I apologize; it's just that I get these," *she raised her hand over her head,* "same old come on lines." *The guy who had first offered her a cart continued to stand by the door.*

"I'm sure. I mean, I understand," *he corrected, sounding a little uneasy. He stood aloof while she talked.*

Obviously he wasn't convinced that she wasn't a fruitcake. She sensed his body language and recounted the previous interaction.

"I understand," *he replied, as he nodded in recognition of the games men play} sounding relieved.*

"No hard feelings?" *she asked. She waited for him to offer his name. Either he didn't catch the hint, or he didn't want to give his name. He simply answered,* "No hard feelings."

He shook her hand. His handshake was firm yet gentle, she observed. She looked him in the eyes. For the first time she noticed that he was an extremely handsome man. He was about six two or three she guessed. He wore his hair short, like he'd had a fresh haircut. His eyes were brown with a twinkle. It was as though he smiled with his eyes instead of his lips. There was something special about him.

"I still need help with selecting a cantaloupe if you don't mind?"

"Of course not; I'd love to."

With her finger on her bottom lip, she looked over the cantaloupe before picking up one.

"You see this one, it's too soft. The meat will be soft and on the mushy side."

Picking up another she explained, "Now this is what you should look for—a brownish, beige color; firm to the touch."

He took it out of her hand, placed it in his cart, and thanked her.

"I really appreciate your help. I'm sure it's going to be sweet."

"Glad I was able to help, ah . . ." She waited for him to add his name. Once again he didn't take the hint or he deliberately ignored it. He nodded his head as if to close the conversation. Strangely, she sensed he was teasing her, but then again she'd been wrong before. Oh well, she thought disappointedly as she turned to finish her shopping. This is not the way I wanted this encounter to end.

As she walked away there was a little sadness in her heart. It troubled her, especially since this was the first time she had ever seen this young man. He didn't even have the decency to give his name.

She remembered her need for salad dressing and headed toward a store clerk.

"Marilyn!" He called over her shoulder.

Her heart skipped a beat. Encouraged but not trying to show it she turned slowly.

"Yes?" she asked in a nonchalant tone.

"Benjamin Reed."

She didn't understand.

"My name is Benjamin Reed." Did she detect a smirk on his face?

She nodded as he stepped closer and continued.

"I work weekends; ten to six at the mechanic shop across the street," he said, pointing. "Maybe I'll see you around sometime?"

"Maybe," she replied, as she tried to sound casual but hoped her voice wouldn't give her away. All the while she tried to find a reason to take her car to the auto shop in the near future.

She was surprised at the way she was acting. Never before had she made an attempt to get to know a guy first. Having been so busy with work after graduating from high school, she rarely dated. She had always dreamed of being a successful business woman. There were some things she wanted to accomplish before getting involved in a relationship.

She put the groceries away and pulled an index card out of the recipe box. After three tries she found a pen that would write. In bold print she wrote:

Mel's Dry Cleaner
Saturday morning

She placed it under the magnet on the refrigerator door. She opened the fridge and peered inside. Nothing seemed appealing. She had planned to fix a salad, but her appetite had changed. She picked up *the carton of orange juice and poured some in a glass, then returned the juice to the fridge. She closed the door and smiled as she looked at the note.*

Usually she hated laundry day. She hated going to the Laundromat and dropping things off at the cleaners. She often told her friends that one day she would have a maid to do all of those tedious things. But tonight was different. She actually was looking forward to going to the cleaners. She smiled as she caught herself humming a tune as she separated the clothes by colors. She could hardly wait until morning. She hoped she would see Benjamin.

Before going to bed, she sorted her clothes for the cleaners. There were only two pieces that needed cleaning: a gray skirt and a white silk blouse. Normally she waited until she had at least ten items but this would have to do.

She folded them up and placed them on the chair in the bedroom near the window. Noticing that it was after ten she set her clock for nine. With pajamas, head scarf and cold cream she headed for the bathroom. She laid her things on the sink and went back to the kitchen.

Marilyn took the card off the refrigerator and with a piece of tape from the dispenser, she taped it to her bedroom mirror—not that she needed a reminder. She noticed that it was getting late, she hurried to get ready for bed.

Saturday morning, she was up before dawn with an unusual amount of energy. Usually, she slept in on the weekend, but not today. She had to take the clothes to the cleaners. She hummed as she prepared a light breakfast. She added milk, sugar and butter to her oatmeal. It was the way her granny had taught her. It always warmed her body and soul. It always brought back memories of the summers she spent with granny and grandpa as a child. To make it even more special and to Marilyn's satisfaction; her granny would add lots of raisins. The oatmeal was always perfect. Never too hot or too cold. Never too gummy or too soupy.

"Man," she murmured as she opened the cabinet for her raisins.

There were a couple of cans of peaches and fruit cocktail, a box of prunes, but no raisins. Marilyn picked up the box of prunes. For a split second she thought of dicing them up in her cereal. After all, raisins and prunes were similar; one was dried grapes and the other dried plums. She quickly decided against it. She considered adding canned peaches then changed her mind. No need to mess up a good bowl of cereal experimenting. She'd just have to eat it without raisins this morning. That reminded her she had to get to the cleaners; it was twenty minutes to ten.

With her dry cleaning folded over her arms, she looked across the street at the mechanic shop and closed her car door. There were several young men out front buying coffee and donuts off a vending truck. Benjamin was not among them.

She dropped her head when she realized that she had caught their attention. They started the usual male theatrics. She was a little embarrassed that they had caught her staring. She hurried inside the building. Safe inside away from the wolf whistles, she glanced out of the window. It was 10:15, still no sight of Benjamin.

His co-workers however were watching the door of the cleaners.

No doubt there would be more of the same. Hopefully their break would be ending soon, until then, she would have to stall.

Fortunately for her she knew Pat, the cashier. It would be easy killing time inside. Having been high school classmates, they made small talk about the five years since graduation. Each were looking forward to their tenth year class reunion, and seeing others they hadn't seen since graduation. Some of the names Pat called Marilyn remembered; others she didn't.

With little in common, they soon ran out of stuff to talk about. She noticed the workers were still out front and concluded that either they were on lunch or their employer was extremely lenient with breaks. Either way she couldn't hide in the cleaners forever.

She checked her receipt and noticed the ten-percent discount she received for paying up front. She folded it and shoved it down in her back pocket. Out the window she could see the guys standing around the truck laughing and talking. She looked around. There was no other exit.

As she watched the guys through the window in a huddle playfully throwing punches she decided to make a run for it. With her eyes on them she pulled open the door. She sized up the distance to her car. It was parked about thirty feet away.

She stepped out of the doorway and bumped into Ben, who was carrying an armful of clothes.

"Oh, I'm sorry," she apologized feeling clumsy.

Looking up into Benjamin's smiling face and seeing the clothes on the ground, she knew that the right thing to do was to pick them up. However, the wrong thing was to bend at the same time that he did. Thump! They bumped heads.

Both stood up holding their heads. Together they broke out into laughter.

Marilyn stopped laughing abruptly. Clearing her throat, in a voice slightly above a whisper, she announced, "We have an audience." Holding her hand close to her chest she nodded her head, pointing across the street.

Ben looked up and waved; they stared. He flashed a broad grin, tipped his cap at the guys, and escorted Marilyn over to her car.

Not knowing what else to say she blurted out, "You're late aren't you?" Oops! Now he knew she had planned her trip to the cleaners.

Catharine Ingram

"Were you looking for me?" he asked with a gleam in his eye.

"Well, I, uh, I," was all she managed to stammer before being interrupted.

"Hey, Ben!" yelled one of the guys from across the street, cupping his hand to his mouth, "Introduce us to your friend." The other guys encouraged him also.

"Alright guys, the show is over. Go on back to work."

Before they could respond the bell rang and ended their break.

"Well, were you looking for me?" he asked not letting her off the hook. Quickly she changed the subject.

"I brought some things to the cleaners," she informed him and pulled the receipt out of her back pocket. Proudly she held it up. He didn't buy it, but no need to push the issue.

"I normally work ten to six, but my mom needed me to run some errands this morning. My father has been sick for a couple of weeks, so I help out as much as I can. I switched with one of the guys, so today I'll start at one."

Puzzled she looked at her watch. He explained. "I'm here to drop these off and pick up my parents' laundry," he explained, as he pulled his crumbled up receipt out of his shirt pocket.

"I'll just be a moment," he continued as he rushed inside the building. Marilyn looked up and smiled as the sun beamed down and warmed her face. The sun felt great, but the real reason for the smile was Benjamin. It was something about him that made her heart flutter. He had her all nervous and giggly like a teenager instead of a twenty-three year old woman. It felt good. It felt right.

In a few minutes Benjamin returned with a pile of clothes slung on his back. It was more than Marilyn had cleaned in a whole year. Seeing the look on her face Benjamin explained. "They only do this twice a year. These are their summer dress clothes. Everything else, my mom irons. Pass me the keys out of the ignition, please?"

The car window was down, but instead of reaching through it, Marilyn opened the door. She took the keys out and walked to the back of the car. Benjamin pointed out the key for the trunk.

"Thanks for the help. I had intended to take all of those things out before I left home." he said. He held the clothes while she rearranged the ice scrape, books and some other things he had in the trunk.

"You are welcome," she assured him, as she spread out the clothes to minimize wrinkles.

"It's late for breakfast and early for lunch, but, if it's okay with you, I'd like to treat you to a cup of coffee or soda," he said, catching her off guard.

"To show my appreciation for the help, of course," he added smiling.

"I'll take a cola," she suggested and pointed across the street to a neighborhood diner. Although she felt comfortable with him, she still didn't know him.

They waited for the traffic to clear before crossing the street. Benjamin chatted about the guys across the street while Marilyn wondered would they soon run out of things to talk about. Her worry was needless. After an hour of enjoyable conversation over soft drinks, they exchanged phone numbers. There was no mention of dating, but in her heart she knew they would be seeing each other again. There was such a connection between the two of them. She didn't know how to explain it. Just call it an intuition.

Chapter Six

Two weeks passed. No phone call. Three weeks passed. No phone call. Marilyn was beginning to think that maybe she had misunderstood Ben. Then on the fifteenth, one month and three days from the day they first met, the phone rang.

"Hi Marilyn, this is Benjamin," he said. Not that he needed to; after all, how many people sound like Barry White?

"Hi, how are you?" she asked trying to sound cool and aloof, while her heart was skipping beats.

"I had wanted to call you two weeks ago and invite you to our bowling tournament, but I couldn't find the little piece of paper with your number on it." He chuckled and continued "I guess it was for the best. I played the worst game I've played all season. But I have to admit it wasn't all my fault."

She didn't understand.

"Don't hang up, Marilyn. This is not a line. I promise. But I just couldn't concentrate. All I could think about was you."

Something in his voice said he wasn't trying to, as her dad used to warn, "run a game or open your nose." There was a grin on her face and a smile in her heart.

"Are you there?" he asked. She hadn't said a word since saying hello.

"I'm here."

"How about dinner and a movie?" he asked.

"Thanks, but I've eaten?" She noticed it was 4:05 and explained. "I was busy mopping and ironing this morning. I worked through lunch so I had an early dinner."

"Okay, maybe some other time," he responded with disappointment in his voice.

"Well, just because I've had dinner doesn't mean we can't catch a good movie. Which one did you have in mind?"

With excitement that he didn't try to hide he stammered out, "Great! Whatever you want to see is fine with me."

"There's a western playing over at the Woods Plaza on Sixty-Third Street. I noticed the marquee this morning." She hoped he liked westerns.

"Are you kidding? This is too good to be true. A beautiful woman who enjoys westerns."

"Hold on, while I get the paper," implored Marilyn.

Separating the paper on the kitchen table, she looked for the movie section. Finding it, she smiled as she noticed an 8:15 show. It would give her plenty of time to put her plan into action.

Picking up the receiver she asked, "How about the one at 8:15? I wouldn't want to be out too late."

"What time should I pick you up?"

"I'll meet you there around five after eight. I need to pick up some things at the Plaza anyway," she informed.

This was their first date. She didn't know a lot about him. Although she believed they would be seeing a lot of each other, she still had to be cautious.

"Is that okay?" she asked, hoping that she hadn't offended him.

"That's fine. See you around eight."

"Hey," she heard him call, just before she placed the phone on the receiver.

"Yes?"

"Call me, Ben."

"Huh?"

"Call me Ben. It's short and to the point, sort of like me," he kidded. "Benjamin sounds so formal."

A picture of Benjamin Franklin with a wig signing the Declaration of Independence flashed before her.

She giggled.

"What's funny?"

"Nothing," she insisted.

"Come on, no secrets."

"Okay, promise to tell you later."

"Promise?"

"Promise!"

Marilyn hung up. Marilyn thought for a moment and picked up the phone. She called her best friend, Nikki.

'Hi Nikki, are you busy tonight?"

"And what makes you think I don't have a date for tonight?" asked Nikki.

"I'm sorry; do you?" said Marilyn.

"No, I don't, but you don't have to act like it's not a possibility," she deadpanned, sounding offended, before she broke out into a loud laugh.

"Gotcha, didn't I?" Nikki teased. They had been friends since high school and although they lived on the same blocks sometime they would go months without seeing each other. However, they always called.

They were as close as any two sisters.

"What's up, my friend?" Nikki asked.

"Girl! You play too much."

"I know, I know. What's up about tonight?"

"Ben. You know, the guy I was telling you about."

"Yes, the one who thought you were a little wacko in the supermarket?"

"Yeah, yeah, that one; he called. We are going to the movies tonight."

"Sorry, I can't do it," Nikki replied.

"Do what?" Marilyn asked puzzled.

"Be a third wheel. I'm from the old school. I believe two is still company, and three is still a crowd."

"Girl, shut up and listen. This is what I want you to do," Marilyn commanded as she spelled out her plan. She and Nikki would take a *cab to the theater. They would meet afterward and she'd offer her a ride home.*

Nikki assured her that she could count on her.

Marilyn folded the newspaper and dropped it in the garbage. She pushed her chair under the table as she pondered what she would wear. The forecast predicted rain. She'd have to remember to take her umbrella.

The phone rang.

It was Nikki.

"I just want you to know I don't have a date for this evening. But guess what? Would you believe that Anthony and I are back together?"

That was good news to Marilyn. She had known Anthony since junior high. They had been in the same homeroom class and often met at the neighborhood library after school to do their homework. Math was her strongest subject and English was his.

They often tutored each other. Knowing that Nikki was failing English and unable to really help her, she introduced her to Anthony who was able to help her pull her D up to a C. Marilyn thought they would make a great couple. However, at the time they both were dating other people.

After graduation, Donna, Anthony's girlfriend, went off to study at Harvard. Being able to come home only for Thanksgiving and Christmas, their relationship slowly deteriorated. They agreed to breakup, promising to remain friends. In less than a year, Anthony and Nikki were dating.

"He said that he'd made up his mind that I wasn't the girl for him after I told him that I wouldn't be pressured into taking this relationship to the next level. Actually what I told him was the only next level in this relationship would come after we had both said I DO."

She laughed. "I can't get with guys who say they are in love with you; they say you are the o-n-l-y one for them; they are ready for all the fringe benefits but they are just not ready for marriage." She laughed. "I told him you have the wrong one, baby. After that he got kind of quiet. I told him I was N-O-T trying to pressure him into anything. I told him I was convinced that he was the guy I wanted to spend the rest of my life with, but if he didn't feel the same, well, no hard feelings. I gave him his ring back and was prepared to go on with my life. I have to admit, my heart was broken but you know what? My self-respect was intact.

"So, what happened then?" Marilyn asked curiously. "Girl, I didn't hear from him for a whole week. Would you believe that he said that even his mom said he needed to call me. He said that he was so moody, his mom threatened to call me if he didn't call. Isn't that sweet?"

"Now, you know I agree with you. Let's face it. We both made some dumb mistakes in college trying to hold on to guys on their terms, but you know what they say—when you learn better you do better. If I haven't learned anything else, I've learned one thing—as a child your parents steer your life, but as an adult you take the wheel. Show me where it says you have to let your boyfriend call the shots."

Wanting to hurry the conversation on while trying not to sound insensitive, Marilyn asked, "How is everything?"

"Fine, we went to a late movie last night. He's on a different shift. He doesn't get off until ten now."

"You know he's also in culinary school. He wanted to try out some of his French recipes on me. I agreed to be the guinea pig. I must say we had a lovely evening," she laughed.

Marilyn didn't want to come off as the mother hen, but she didn't like the way this conversation was going. One thing her mom had always stressed: avoid late-night dates. They had a way of being disarming. Not willing to waste any more time or prolong the suspense, Marilyn blurted out, "Please say you didn't do anything stupid, Nikki!"

"I can't say that," her voice dropped. "Unfortunately, I did."

Silence.

Marilyn didn't know what to say.

Nikki broke the silence, "I feel bad. I was weak. I knew it was wrong to have that third slice of pie, but it was my favorite, key lime!"

"You always do that to me. You have a weird sense of humor," Marilyn cried.

Marilyn kept her eye on the clock. She had to get ready for her date with Ben, yet she wanted to be sensitive to Nikki. She knew the break up had been hard on her. Unfortunately, Marilyn's work schedule left little time for socializing. She'd hardly seen Nikki in the last few months.

Marilyn walked inside at 8:05, Ben was waiting. They chatted a moment before purchasing their tickets. The theater was crowded. It was an older quieter group giving way to an enjoyable evening.

After the movie ended, they sat chatting, allowing the other patrons to exit.

Marilyn scanned the aisles looking for Nikki.

"Hey, that's my best friend," she said and waved.

The raised arm caught Nikki's eye, and she waved back.

"Hey you guys; how did you enjoy the movie?"

"Loved it," said Marilyn.

Ben nodded in agreement.

"Are you by yourself?" Marilyn asked as rehearsed.

"Just me, myself and I," Nikki teased.

"We can drop you off," said Marilyn looking at Ben for confirmation.

"Sure."

Chapter Seven

A year later, almost to the day they met, Ben proposed. They enjoyed a short engagement, as they planned a late summer wedding. Two weeks before the big day Marilyn was summoned to jury duty. She was excited. It would be her first time serving. However, her excitement soon faded.

The trial was about domestic abuse. The wife in a wheel chair with healed marks on her face and right arm. She sat with her head down during most of the trial. As the jury watched in horror, the prosecutor showed over twenty graphic pictures of cuts and welts on different parts of her body.

The defendant was very active in his family's lives. He and his wife often volunteered as chaperones for the school. For twenty years he had been a great provider. However, a year earlier he found himself downsized from work and had started drinking. One evening of binge drinking left the family emotionally and physically scarred.

The judge sentenced the father to a year in jail. Their oldest son, overcome with grief by the verdict, rushed to his father's side. Marilyn left believing there was hope for the relationship as she watched the husband and wife exchange glances.

A week later, as they watched an old Western classic on television, Ben noticed that Marilyn was unusually quiet. It was obvious that something was wrong. Not wanting to pry he sat quietly hoping that she would open up. She did.

"Ben, have you ever hit a woman?"

"What, brought that on?" Remembering the trial, he quickly added, "Oh, the trial." Sitting up straight he reached for her hands and held them together. He kissed them gently.

"Marilyn, I love you. I've loved you from the first moment I laid eyes on you. Well, not really the first moment, but the second moment, after I found out you weren't a little loony," he added wanting to make her smile.

It worked. She smiled, remembering that first day in the produce section.

"I'm serious," she said and pushed in his chest.

"Ouch, you hurt me," he joked as he held his chest.

Seeing the conversation was going nowhere she jumped up. He grabbed her hand and pulled her back to the couch.

"All kidding aside," he paused and searched for the right words.

"Marilyn, I love you. I would do nothing to hurt you. I'd rather walk away than to cause you physical or emotional pain. It would be hard to live with myself if I made one tear fall from your eyes."

She forced a weak smile and nodded. He pulled her close, put his arm around her, and whispered "I want to be the best husband there ever was. I want you to be the happiest bride." He kissed her on the forehead and leaned backs on the couch.

"What's wrong? What are you thinking?" she asked sheepishly.

"I was just thinking of all the reasons I love you. You're kind, considerate, thoughtful, loving; you're strong yet soft; tenderhearted; and you're sensitive."

"Thank you, that's sweet," she said as she leaned forward and kissed him.

"Oh, one more, one more," he added and held up a finger up a finger, "you are passionate!"

Ben noticed the time. It was 11:12.

*"I have to get out of here. You are **not** my bride yet. Soon, but not yet."*

As he stood, he helped her up. They walked hand in hand to the door. He turned and brushed a tear from her cheek. He took her arms and wrapped them around his neck. He confessed, "You have me hooked, and I'm one happy fish."

She blushed and dropped her head.

"Goodnight," he said and blew her a kiss. She pretended to reach out and grab it as she closed the door. She felt like a princess as she laid her head against the door. She held his kiss close to her heart. She daydreamed of being married to Ben, a loving, caring, and hard-working man. He was a real gentleman.

Marilyn smiled as she walked into the living room and flopped down on the couch. She couldn't think of one negative thing about Ben. Yet, with one of her neighbors being abused and with the trial fresh in her mind she was perplexed. For the first time she could remember, her heart and mind were out of sync. She had to talk to someone.

She picked up the phone and dialed the same seven digits she always dialed when she needed advice. Seven, five, nine . . . . She noticed the clock on the television. It was 11:21 p.m. Aunt Liz had been in bed hours ago. Quickly she hung up the phone. No need to scare her calling this late. She'd call first thing in the morning.

7:15 the phone rang. It was Uncle Robert.

"Hello," answered Marilyn, as she turned the clock on the nightstand around. Who would be calling this early? It was only five after seven.

"Baby Girl, hope I didn't wake you? I went fishing, yesterday," he did not wait for a response but continued. "I caught some nice hand-size perch and I have some buffalo. I thought you might want some before I start giving them away."

"Thanks Uncle Robert, I'll take a few of the perch. You know I don't fool with buffalo after what happened last summer," she reminded him.

He had forgotten all about the fish-fry at their neighbors. Marilyn had a scary call when a small fish bone became lodged in her throat. For a moment she was convinced that her life was ending as memories of her childhood literally flashed before her eyes. She vowed to never touch buffalo again.

She threw the comforter back and reached for her robe. There was a chill in the room. The slight movement of the sheers reminded her that she had left the window up. Although she lived on the third floor, she never liked to leave her windows open at night. She closed the window and noticed drapes were damp from the rain.

It had been one of those quiet rains that, unless one had looked out she would not have known that it had rained. There had been no lightning or thunder. It had been the kind of rain that was serene and peaceful and lured one to sleep in the daytime.

"I'll drop them off after I come back from the grocery store. Your Auntie forgot to pick up some half and half. She knows I don't drink any coffee without cream."

"That will be fine," Marilyn said.

Uncle Robert wasn't paying attention. He continued, "I think she's trying to get me to stop drinking coffee, but I'm not." Marilyn knew from the way he was talking that her aunt was sitting nearby. He was really talking to her instead of Marilyn. It was just safer this way.

He continued, "She talked me into giving up pork because of my blood pressure, but there's nothing wrong with a cup of coffee in the morning.

Do you see anything wrong with it?" he asked, wanting Marilyn to weigh in. It was a set-up, and she wasn't going to take the bait.

"I'm going to be out your way around noon tomorrow, so I'll pick them up. Thanks Uncle Robert." She'd learned her lesson well in the past. Never get between them when they are arguing. The one thing you didn't want to do was take either side.

"Uncle Robert, I need to speak with Aunt Liz if she's up."

She knew that Aunt Liz was up, and if she were a gambling woman she'd put her money on the fact that she had been in the room the whole time he was talking to her.

"She's sitting right in front of me looking down my throat." Uncle Robert said. Marilyn smiled at his saying.

"You can drink all the coffee you want, old man. I'm just trying to look out for you," Aunt Liz said in the background.

Marilyn smiled, glad that she was on the phone instead of being at their house for this argument. They were the kind of couple that played one minute and fussed the next. Marilyn had to admit it was obvious they were very much in love. They were the kind of couple who did everything together. Uncle Robert would even take Aunt Liz on his weekend fishing trips.

"Hi Marilyn," said Aunt Liz as she took the phone from Uncle Robert.

"Auntie, how did you know Uncle Robert was the man for you?"

"Child, I didn't know that Robert was the man for me," she kidded.

Something about the way she said it gave her away. Marilyn knew that she was needling Uncle Robert. In the background, she heard him respond.

"I didn't see anybody else knocking your door down to marry you," he retaliated. He chuckled, "Unless you're going to count Slump-back

Henry. Slump-back Henry Johnson. He was so old you were going to have to carry him over the threshold."

"Go on to the store, old man," she replied, laughing.

"Bring me some pop back."

"What kind?" she heard him ask.

"Diet pop! I don't want to be fat like you."

"Too late," he shot back.

Laughing she asked, "How you doing, Baby Girl? I'm sorry to keep you waiting. You know your uncle."

"Auntie, I'm not sure I'm ready for marriage."

"Oh child, don't listen to your uncle and me," she warned thinking that their antics worried Marilyn. "We were just fooling around. We really do love each other."

"I know. It's not you guys. It's that," she searched for the right words. "What if it doesn't work? What if we stop loving each other?"

"Look Baby, there are no guarantees in life. God doesn't show you the whole picture. I used to think it would be nice if He did, but I've learned better. I no longer think so. Some things would make us anxious. We would want to fast forward. Some would paralyze us, hinder us from moving. All I can tell you is that you just have to trust your heart. Baby, follow it!"

Marilyn was quiet and pondered her aunt's words. She was sure her heart was saying Ben is the one.

"Are you okay, baby?" her aunt asked during the silence.

"I'm fine. Thanks." Her aunt's words were few but spoke volumes.

"Alright, baby girl, I have to put this man's coffee on before he gets back from the store. I don't want to have to go upside his head."

"I'll pick up the fish tomorrow," Marilyn reminded her.

She hung up the phone and laughed as she tried to picture her aunt and uncle fighting. Even though they were always cracking on each other they were always touching. Marilyn would go over, and find Aunt Liz giving him a back rub or he would be cutting her toenails.

Marilyn laughed as she remembered the last time she had gone over for dinner. It had stormed. As soon as they finished dessert the lights went off.

Aunt Liz said, "I hope we have some matches around here." Immediately Uncle Robert responded, "I have some right here in my pocket." Aunt Liz shot back, "Am I married to a closet smoker or an arsonist? You always have matches."

They lit some candles and moved to the living room.

The lights came on, and it was time for round two.

Uncle Robert commented that a cup of coffee would be nice.

Aunt Liz responded. "I told you he was backwards. Coffee keeps everybody awake. Not him, though. It helps him to sleep like a baby. Now tell me if something isn't wrong with that man?" she quipped as she went into the kitchen.

Marilyn thanked Uncle Robert for such a great meal and promised to invite them over as soon as she learned how to cook like Aunt Liz.

"Well, I guess that won't be any time soon. Only a few are as great a cook as my little woman," he whispered, "but don't tell her I said it."

"Mum's the word," Marilyn promised.

"What's the word?" asked Aunt Liz coming in from the kitchen. She carried a tray with two cups of coffee and a cup of cocoa. She passed the cocoa to Marilyn and a cup of coffee to Uncle Robert. She sat her cup on the table and walked towards the kitchen.

Uncle Robert stirred the coffee and smiled approvingly at the rich color. Convinced that it had the right amount of cream, he put the cup close to his nose and inhaled the rich, fresh aroma. He smiled and called to get her attention.

"Liz."

"Yes?" she asked, as she stopped at the kitchen door.

He made a giant check mark in the air and smiled approvingly. He took a sip and shouted, "Liz, this is instant coffee!"

"I know it."

As she looked on, he took an imaginary eraser, erased the check and replaced it with a giant X. She shook her head.

With her hand on her hip she confessed, "I only fix you fresh perk in the mornings. Most of the time I give you a cup of instant when you want coffee at night." She shook her head. "After all these years, now his taste buds want to start working."

She took the tray into the kitchen. She returned and sat next to Uncle Robert.

"I think I'll have a couple of cookies with mine. What about you guys?" Marilyn asked, as she headed to the kitchen. They declined.

Marilyn took two cookies canister. She pulled a chair from the table. The kitchen felt warm. Not the kind of warm from the oven but the kind that made you feel good. The kind that made you feel safe. The kind that made you feel loved.

She sat back and listened to them. It was obvious they enjoyed each other's company very much. She smiled as they continued to go back and forth ribbing each other in the living room.

"I guess it wasn't too bad," said Aunt Liz; she noticed that his cup was empty.

"I guess it was okay after all," he conceded. "I've learned to take what I can get and make the best out of it," he dropped his head and pretended to be sad. She moved the pillow over and sat on the couch beside him.

"The way my ankle has been bothering me today, you had better be grateful for what you got."

He scooted to the end of the couch. She looked at him with disbelief. He reached for her leg and placed it across his lap. He slipped off her house shoes and began to massage her toes and ankle. He then began massaging her shin and calf.

"It's my ankle where the pain is, Robert," she informed him with a smile.

"Sorry, I didn't know whether or not the pain was traveling."

"You are not that slick, old man. However, I do believe in rewarding one for their effort." Playfully, Robert's face lit up as Aunt Liz shrugged her shoulders and confessed, "I guess it's just the teacher in me."

Marilyn mopped the floor around the window and wiped off the window sill. She looked forward to cooking the fresh fish. The frozen fish in the market never tasted as good as what Uncle Robert would catch. She put the mop away and pulled out her senior summer vacation scrapbook.

It was buried under some old magazines in the closet. Several pictures that were not glued fell to the floor. She sat on the floor as she picked them up. There were several pictures of her parents with Uncle Robert and Aunt Liz. The pictures had been taken at their family reunion the year she graduated from high school. The family had rented a van and had driven to New Orleans. Along the way they had stopped for a picnic lunch at a beautiful roadside park. It was her favorite family memory.

Marilyn searched through the photos. She was mostly interested in the photos of Uncle Robert and Aunt Liz. In each photo they looked the happy couple. Most were candid shots. Holding up one she smiled and put the scrapbook back in the closet. It was a picture Marilyn had taken of Uncle Robert with his arm around Aunt Liz as they slept in the van.

Marilyn had grown up in a house filled with love. She knew her parents absolutely adored each other, but there was something different about her Aunt and Uncle's relationship. Uncle Robert always teased and said it was because Aunt Liz knew he would go up side her head if she got out of line. Aunt Liz had confided in her that their marriage hadn't always been good. She admitted that they had to allow the Lord to teach them how to relate to one another. One thing Marilyn knew, their home now, was always filled with joy.

Chapter Eight

She laid the photo on the end table and reached for the phone.

"Hi, Ben. It's Marilyn," she announced joyfully.

"Hi, what's up?" he asked, pleased yet surprised she had called.

"Nothing. Just wondering, do we still have an in-home movie date?"

They rarely went out on weekends. They chose to spend them alone watching old movies on the television. She would buy pops and put them in the freezer for a couple of hours to become slushy and pop a large bowl of popcorn.

Marilyn owned a popcorn popper. It was a gift she received from the bank after opening her checking account. It was still in the box. She preferred to pop the popcorn with a little oil in a heavy skillet with a pot turned down on it. That was the way her mom did it when she was growing up.

"I sure hope so," he added, remembering how quiet she was the night before.

"I'm on my way to mom. I'll see you around 7:15. Okay?" he asked.

There was a noticeable difference in her voice. It was almost as if he could hear her smiling.

"It's that . . . . it's that I miss you," she confessed.

There was silence. He expressed a sigh of relief. "You had me worried there for a moment. After last night I thought this might be a Dear John phone call."

She knew what he meant. She tried to play it down.

"You can't get rid of me that easy," she assured him. "It's too late. You are stuck with me now," she added.

"And I couldn't be happier!"

"Ben?"

"Yes?"

She hesitated.

She picked up the picture again and smiled. It was as if a light bulb had gone off in her head. She knew the secret to a good relationship. Her parents knew it and so did Uncle Robert and Aunt Liz. The key ingredient was friendship mixed with respect, love and a great sense of humor.

She smiled as she remembered something her Aunt Bea had said about marriage. It happened about a year after her brother, Uncle Willie, divorced his wife, Aunt Mildred, and remarried a much younger, thinner model type. At their first year anniversary dinner someone had been overheard snickering about how the streamline jet that had replaced Mildred had suddenly turned into a Boeing 747.

That remark prompted Aunt Bea to warn "Never marry someone just because they are rich in stocks and bonds, the market can crash in a day. Never marry someone just because they have a great job, companies downsize all the time. Never marry just because the man is a hunk or the woman is a 10 because the hunk can become a lump and the 10 can become a 20 before you know it."

"Marilyn, are you there?" Ben asked.

"*Yes, I'm here. I was just thinking about some words of wisdom my Aunt Bea gave me.*"

"*Is everything okay?*" *he asked concerned.*

"*No, everything is not OKAY,*" *she said with her voice dropping and then quickly rising.* "*Everything is GREAT!*"

"*Good,*" *he said exhaling a sigh of relief.* "*I'll see you later.*"

Raising the plastic, she placed the picture back in the album. Instead of putting the album back in the closet, she left it out to show Benjamin some of the great shots she had taken of the city of New Orleans.

Chapter Nine

Marilyn woke up around two in the morning with an ache in her neck. The couch was nice for sitting, but it was uncomfortable for sleeping. The first thought on her mind was the twins. It was going to be a dull weekend without them. They brought so much joy to her life.

She wondered what Benjamin was doing. Did he miss her? Was he okay? After much twisting and turning she found a comfortable position. Why bother going to bed? She would be getting up in a couple of hours.

Listening closely, she could hear a faint scratching sound coming from the back. She recognized the sound. The fan in the twins' room was on. The oscillating fan was blowing against the African beaded wall rug. The breeze blowing against the beads made a soft cutting sound.

It reminded her of an incident years earlier.

Reggie was about four. She was awakened one morning by sounds coming from the kitchen. It was 4:12 in the morning. Quickly she got out of the bed and slipped her feet into her slippers. She had informed the landlord about a mouse in the kitchen a few weeks earlier. She hoped it wasn't back.

Of all nights, Ben wasn't home. Just for tonight he was working the graveyard shift. Noticing a chill in the room she grabbed her robe off the foot of the bed. She entered the kitchen and found Reggie sitting at the table eating cereal. He looked up and smiled when she entered the room.

"Mama. I'm a big boy. I fixed my own food!" he shouted proudly.

"What are you doing?" she asked, noticing two opened boxes of cereal spilled all over the table and milk gushing out of the carton on the floor. Picking up the milk, she smelled gas. On the stove was a skillet with a piece of cheese and two slices of bread. The burner was partially on. Gas was seeping out.

"Haven't I told you not to mess with the stove," Marilyn scolded before turning off the burner.

"I'm a big boy, mommy. I fixed my own food."

Recognizing that he was trying to be helpful, she gave him a hug.

"Yes, you are mommy's big boy." She tried to sound cheerful, but he had given her a terrible scare. Had she not awakened it could have been a tragedy. She had warned him several times about the danger of the stove. The thought of a different outcome left her shaken.

As she cleaned up the mess, he sat on the edge of the chair and ate his cereal. His head rocked from side to side. With his feet dangling, he softly hummed along with the Sesame Street characters. He was a picture of innocence.

Later that afternoon while planning dinner, Marilyn remembered that Reggie had spilled the milk she needed to make macaroni and cheese, and she would have to run to the store. Also remembering that she needed toothpaste, tissue and shoe polish, she made a list.

As they entered the store, Reggie started yelling, "I want to ride!"

"Okay, okay I hear you," she assured him and pulled out a cart. She picked him up and placed his feet through the spaces. He was happy and she was relieved. Twice in the last month he had wandered off, in a frenzy as she had rushed up and down the aisles looking for him. Each time she had found him playing in the revolving door.

As she pushed the cart down the milk aisle, Reggie kicked a lady as she passed by pushing a cart with a little girl. He licked his tongue out at the little girl. She began to cry. The lady pulled off her sunglasses in disbelief. She picked up her child and whispered some words of comfort.

"Stop that, that's not nice. Say you are sorry," Marilyn insisted.

Reggie looked on, smiling.

"Say you are sorry, young man," Marilyn insisted.

He dropped his head and held the rim of the cart.

"I'm sorry," she apologized to the woman not knowing what else to say. The woman brushed the footprints off her white slacks and gave Reggie a cold look. She shook her head and continued down the aisle without saying another word.

"I'm not going to take you to McDonald's."

"Um-hum."

"No, I'm not."

"Yes, you is."

"That's yes you are, and no, I'm not."

"I want to go to McDonald's. I want to go to McDonald's!" he started crying out louder and louder.

"If you are a good boy I'll take you," she pleaded with him.

"I'll be a good boy, mommy."

The store was crowded. Noticing that the toothpaste was in the next aisle, she decided to leave the cart. She would run over and get it. It would save time and the hassle of maneuvering the cart.

As she picked up two tubes of toothpaste, she heard a familiar, loud cry. Fearful of what had happened, she hurried back to her cart.

Reggie was hollering to the top of his voice as she rounded the corner. "What's wrong, baby?" she pleaded, thinking that he was crying because she had left him for a few moments.

He pointed down the aisle. "That lady pinched me on my leg." Furious, Marilyn looked down the aisle. There were only two teenage boys looking at boxes of cereal.

One walked over to Marilyn. "Ma'am your son pulled a little girl's hair, and when her mom told him to stop he kicked at the mom." The young man was finding it hard not to laugh. "That's when the mom pinched his leg."

Marilyn noticed Reggie holding his leg. She raised his pant and gasped as she stared at the purple welt. She continued to interrogate the teens. What did the lady look like? What was she wearing? All they could tell her was that the lady was wearing white slacks and had on sunglasses.

Like a mad lady, Marilyn pushed her cart up and down every aisle{and looked for the lady. She was no where to be found. Marilyn headed to the front of the store.

"My leg hurt, Mommy!" he cried.

"It's going to be alright," she promised as she dried his eye and scanned the parking lot for the lady. She noticed her watch and headed to the checkout counter.

His crying stopped, and his face lit up immediately. His eyes dotted up and down the shelves of candies and gums. Before she could open her mouth he had grabbed a package from the shelf. She was in no mood for a fight. She had purposely avoided going down the cookies and candy aisle. Marketing experts, she thought. They know how to get you. Put the sweet stuff in a place where you can't bypass it.

Behind her another mother was going through the same thing with her set of toddlers. They quieted down only after the mother promised to take them to the clown's place for burgers and fries.

Seeing her son today brought Marilyn little comfort. The thought of Reggie being away from home for eighteen months really grieved her spirit. It wasn't the couch that caused Marilyn's discomfort. She was restless. Several episodes from the past flooded her memory. In retrospect, each one had been a red flag going up.

However, they went unchecked.

Two weeks after Reggie started in the fourth grade, Miss Wallace, his teacher, requested a conference with Marilyn. At 2:45 p.m. Marilyn pulled into the parking lot. She was tired. The day had been long and exhausting. For a moment she just sat in her car with the motor running, she dreaded getting out. It was going to be the same old thing. Your child did this, your child did that. It was ways her child. Sure her child was a little spoiled but so were some of the other students. Her baby was only nine and in the fourth grade. How bad could he be?

As she walked into the office, Mrs. Morris, the assistant principal, looked up.

"Good afternoon, Mrs. Reed. Miss Dean is expecting you in room 104. It's the first door to your right after you pass the library."

With a simple thank-you, she walked out of the office but not before overhearing Mrs. Morris say to the office clerk, "It's going to be a very l-o-n-g year."

As she walked down the hall she became furious wit the whole school system. Every time she looked around someone was asking her to come to the school. Her baby wasn't any worst than the rest of the children. She was getting tired of everybody acting like her child was the problem.

As she opened the door, an elderly lady at the desk stood up and extended her hand.

"Hi, I'm Miss Dean. I will be your child's teacher for the next three or four weeks. I don't know whether or not you are aware of it, but Mrs. Wallace, your child's regular teacher, will be off for medical reasons."

Noticing the frown on Marilyn's face she continued, "Have a seat, please. I'll try to make this brief."

"This is not something that I usually have to do, that is, call a parent about her or his child's behavior. However, your child is an exception."

"Mrs. Reed, I've taught elementary education for 34 years, and your son is the first child that I . . . well, let's just say he's the first child that I've taught that makes me want to shake him. He's a bully, he's bossy and he doesn't respect authority."

Marilyn's mouth dropped. She couldn't believe what she had just heard.

"I'm just being real. The reason I can be real is because I'm not worried about losing my job. I'm retiring in three months. I'm sixty-three, most of my life is behind me, but you and your son on the other hand have a whole life before you. Don't blow it."

Marilyn was furious. How dare she try to tell her how to raise her son!

Mrs. Dean continued, "Mrs. Reed, I'm concerned about your son. There's some issues here. Have you ever considered counseling?"

Before the words were out of her mouth Marilyn was on her feet in defense, "Mrs. Dean, no disrespect, but my child is fine. Is it possible that the problem lies with you instead of Reggie? Could it be that you are may be too old to deal with an energetic child?"

Mrs. Dean smiled and walked over to the window. She had heard it before. Most parents were the last to recognize their child's cry for help.

"Mrs. Reed, let me share a few things with you. I teach not for the money, I assure you. My husband died a few years ago, and he made sure I was financially secure. I teach for the joy of teaching. So often our children in the inner-city don't get the quality education that they need and deserve. My goal is to make a difference. Let the record show that I have a lot to keep me busy. I'm single-handedly raising my four grandchildren. I can assure you I have the energy."

"I'm sorry. I didn't mean to . . . ."

"No harm done. No offence taken."

Mrs. Dean hesitated before asking, "Is Reggie's father actively involved in his life?" She noticed that Mrs. Reed jaw flinched. Bingo! She knew that she was on to something.

Mrs. Dean waited for her to give some information. She didn't want to pry or force her to shut down. She watched her facial expression as she dropped her head.

"No, he's not involved, and that's okay. I can take care of my son by myself," she insisted.

"I'm sure you can provide him with love, food, clothes and shelter, but he needs his father, grandfather or uncle. He needs that male role model."

"Does his father live in the city? How often does he see him?"

"His father left when he was six."

"What kind of relationship did he have with his father?" she asked, confident that whatever issues Reggie was having stemmed from his father's absence in the home.

"They had a great relationship. As a matter of fact we all did, except when it came to disciplining. He was too strict. He believes in spanking, and I don't." Relaxing, she continued quoting something she had read in a book. *"A spanking is violence and we all know violence begets violence. Children have minds of their own and we have to give them the freedom to express themselves."*

Seeing that the conversation was going no where, Mrs. Dean decided to draw the conversation to a close.

"My, look at the time. I have to pick up my grandchildren from the afternoon program. I've enjoyed talking to you Mrs. Reed." Extending her hand, Mrs. Dean said, "I really would like for us to continue this conversation tomorrow evening if it's okay with you."

Marilyn nodded her head.

"Good, how about 3:30?" she asked looking at her daily planner.

"That will be fine," Marilyn said as she stood up and extended her hand. "I apologize for being rude. I know you have my son's best interest at heart."

"Your son is a handsome, charming young man, but he needs discipline. As a matter of fact, all of us do," she said as she pinched her love handles.

"I know what you mean." They both broke into laughter. Marilyn left feeling good about her visit. She sensed that Mrs. Dean was genuinely concerned about Reggie. She promised to talk with Reggie, and Mrs. Dean agreed to keep her updated on his attitude and performance.

Marilyn's neck was stiff the next morning. It was partly from the long drive, but mostly from sleeping on a too short couch. As she unfolded the news paper she thought of Reggie. The young man she saw yesterday wasn't her baby. He was a stranger. Somewhere in the midst of raising the twins, she had failed her firstborn.

As she poured her coffee the headline caught her attention. It showed a famous couple who had just tied the knot. They looked extremely happy. She remembered the good times that she and Benjamin had enjoyed. She remembered their wedding day.

Their wedding had been straight out of a magazine. It was picture perfect. They were married in the church that Ben had attended all of his life. It was a beautiful sunny day with just enough of a breeze to keep your make-up from running.

The church was large with lots of glass windows which allowed the sun to shine in. Her bridemaids had decorated the sanctuary with lots of white carnations and orchids.

Each pew had a cluster of flowers with a large white bow on each end. There was a light flowery fragrance in the air.

Her maids wore long sleeveless periwinkle dresses with a slight flare.

All of the guys, including the ring bearer, wore white tuxedos with periwinkle cummerbunds. The two flower girls wore long white dresses with head bands of tiny white flowers.

The day had definitely belonged to Marilyn. She wore a long v-neck white satin gown with lace sleeves. Her hair was pulled back in a simple yet chic ball that complimented her veil. It covered her face, yet showed her radiance. To counter Ben's height, Marilyn wore three-inch heels.

As the organist began to play the wedding march, the double doors to the sanctuary opened slowly. There was an "Ahhh" from the audience as Marilyn slowly walked down the aisle on her father's arm. All eyes were on her. Her eyes were on Ben.

Smiling, Marilyn put her glass in the sink as she remembered that she had almost been upstaged by three-year-old Tiffany, the flower girl. She had stolen everyone's heart with her beautiful smile and cute dimples. Unlike the five-year-old ring bearer who cried and had to be coaxed down the aisle, she showed poise. She dropped the flower petals along the runner along the runner and stopped several times to pose for the photographer. She was the talk of the wedding.

Aunt Liz often teased her saying, "Every eye in the church was on the flower girl except Ben's. His eyes never left the door. He was nervously waiting for you to make your entrance. I can see his face now. The moment you walked through the doors his eyes widened. If I never see it again I know what love looks like in a man's eyes. I saw it clearly on your wedding day. You have a good man Marilyn." She pleaded, "Don't take him for granted. Take time to hear him and understand his needs."

With a lump in her throat she choked back tears. She had never seen it coming. She thought they would be together forever. She knew their views were different on parenting. However, on everything else they pretty much agreed.

Marilyn pushed the chair under the table and switched off the light. She decided to get a couple more hours of sleep. Feeling relaxed, she kicked her slippers off and crawled into bed. She fluffed up the pillow and tried to remember when things started to go wrong. It was following Reggie's birth. Their differences in parenting began to put a strain on their marriage.

Before the baby, they had some small disagreements, but it was about the usual stuff, like how much debt they were going to incur fixing up their apartment, and whether or not to buy a new car or a used one. After much discussion they always came to a compromise.

Life was good, but little by little, after the baby, things began to unravel.

Benjamin's parents, Willie and Marva, were excited to be first time grandparents. They flew in from Boston for the baby shower and spared no cost. You would have thought that all the guests had arrived after they finished unloading their luggage. Even they had to acknowledge that maybe . . . just maybe . . . they had gone a little overboard. During their week stay, they volunteered to paint the nursery. For a border Marva asked if she could draw tiny footprints around the room. Marilyn and Ben had planned to do it, but neither had the heart to say no. By the time the baby came the only thing they had to buy was formula.

The summer Reggie turned five, Marilyn's cousin, Mabel, invited them to her mom, Aunt Bea's, eighty-ninth birthday party. She was the oldest living relative. They decided to throw her a bash that would leave the family talking for years to come. Mabel took credit for the party, but actually it had been Aunt Bea's idea.

On the first Monday in June, after going to the doctor for a severe case of heartburn, brought on by eating pickled pig feet and greens, Aunt Bea played the sympathy card like Ray Charles played the piano. She sent out a plea for everyone to come and visit if they wanted to see her one last time. John, Aunt Bea's late husband, had always said that she could con a fox out of his fur in the middle of a Rocky Mountain winter. She knew no one would have the heart to say no. No one would want it said that they had refused a dying woman's last request.

Aunt Bea lived with her youngest son on a large farmhouse nestled way back off the highway, practically surrounded by trees. With no phone (she refused to share a party line with her nosey neighbor), or television (an idiot box with people telling stuff they should be ashamed to even admit to), it was the kids' worse nightmare. The parents on the other hand, looking forward to some peace and quiet, thought it was the ideal place for a vacation.

Mabel had taken her vacation three weeks early and had spared no pain or expense in making her mom's birthday party one that everyone would remember for years. She single-handedly shopped and prepared all the food with the exception of the birthday cake. Aunt Bea insisted that it come from the bakery in nearby Mark City. After all she said, "I didn't live all these years to have a lopsided cake with some crooked letters for my birthday party."

Aunt Bea's body showed signs of age, lots of them but her wit was sharp. She often laughed when babies stared at her. She said they had never seen a chocolate covered raisin so big. She was one of the most confident women in the county. She walked with an air of pride and held her head high like a queen. She heard her mom tell her great grandfather playfully, "her pride could cause her to drown." She said, "If a bad storm comes, the rain is going to fall straight down her nose."

All of her life Aunt Bea had been very active on the farm, in the community, as well as at church. Her dad had always told her that she moved too fast for weight to get a hold on her. Now that arthritis had settled in her joints, she'd slowed down and weight had caught up with her. She was a big woman weighing over two hundred pounds. Every time Mabel took her for a check-up it was the same.

Her doctor would constantly remind her to lose some weight by pushing back from the table, and each time she reminded him that she had seen her three score and ten and whatever else the Good Lord saw fit to give her was okay with her. She would tell him that she met the Lord on the drudge ditch when she was nine while picking black berries. She didn't fear death. She knew that she wasn't perfect, but she had spent her life trying to live the way the Lord said in His Word—The Bible. She told him that she knew it was well with her soul.

He'd just shake his head because he'd been her doctor for over twenty years, and if there was one thing he knew it was once she'd made up her mind about something you might as well give up.

The birthday party had been a memorable one. Aunt Bea was elated to be the center of so much attention. Her strong robust voice could be heard chuckling the whole weekend. Usually she turned in around 8:00 at night and arose around 6:00 in the morning but not this weekend. Not wanting to miss any of the fun she stayed up half of the night, yawning all the way.

The children enjoyed stories of her childhood and they especially loved the ones about their parents. Never in her life could she remember feeling so much love, joy, peace and happiness on the farm. She was overheard telling one of her cousins that she'd had enough fun to take her to her grave. She wouldn't be surprised if her neighbors, the Johnsons on the next farm, could hear all the fun they were having.

Marilyn and Benjamin had been the first to arrive and they were the last to leave. They longed to spend one more night, but the ten-hour drive was a reminder that they needed to be on the move.

Around noon that Sunday as they packed the last of their things, Reggie played with his action figures on the porch steps.

With a big smile on her face Aunt Bea pushed open the screen door, with a large bowl of popcorn in one hand and a tall glass of lemonade in the other. Making small baby steps as to not spill the drink, she slowly made her way to the rocker. She placed her bowl on the table and took a sip of her drink as she sat down. Her weight caused the rocker leg to slide back and sent one of her flowerpots crashing to the ground.

Marilyn and Benjamin were organizing the luggage in the trunk of the car when they heard Aunt Bea raise her voice. Puzzled by her tone, they both looked up.

"Baby, pick that up and put it on the end of the porch," she asked Reggie. No response.

"Baby, pick that pot up and put it on the porch!" she asked, raising her voice.

As she raised her voice, Reggie looked up for a second and then continued to play with his action figures.

"Boy, for you to sit there like you didn't hear me, you must be sick. But that's okay because I'm a baptized sister who believe in healing, and I'm about to lay hands on you!"

She attempted to get up but was stuck in the chair. Reggie looked up and broke out in a loud laughter as he pointed at Aunt Bea. "Mom, look. Look. She's so fa . . ."

"Reggie!" Marilyn stopped him. She couldn't believe what she'd almost heard. She knew he was getting ready to say fat. Her eyes quickly darted over to Aunt Bea. It took all of her energy to refrain from laughing.

Seeing Aunt Bea's bottom wiggling as she struggled to free herself was hilariously funny and a sight to behold.

"Reggie, pick up that flower pot like she asked you," Marilyn insisted as Ben rushed to help Aunt Bea.

Slowly Reggie stood up, looking down with his mouth poked out. Inch by inch, he reluctantly moved over to the pot and in slow motion picked it up. Before Ben reached her, Aunt Bea had freed herself from the chair and stood with her hands on her hips

Her mouth trembled as she tried hard to control her anger. Never had any of her grandchildren or great-nieces or nephews been so disrespectful.

"That child needs to stay with me a couple of weeks. I bet he'd learn how to respect grow-ups," she mumbled under her breath. Frown lines across her forehead revealed a deep concern as she raised her wig up in the front and scratched her head. One of her long white plaits fell loosely down on her ear as she pulled her wig back in place. She turned and headed toward the screen door.

"Ma! Ma! Look!" shouted Reggie as he jumped up and down, pointing toward Aunt Bea. Dangling on the side of her head was the long white plait. It was a sharp contrast with her black wig.

"It's not polite to point," reminded Marilyn as she grabbed his hand and pulled it down. Ben turned around and walked to the trunk of the car.

After rearranging the remaining pieces of luggage, he closed the trunk. Hearing the screen door squeak, they looked up to see Aunt Bea with a clear plastic container filled with cookies. It was Marilyn's favorite *teacakes. Umm, she could imagine the taste of sweet butter and the hint of nutmeg.*

"I thought I could smell fresh-baked cakes in the kitchen this morning. After I didn't see any, I assumed it was from the celebration. When did you bake these, in the middle of the night?"

"I baked them when you all went into town yesterday evening. I put them up so you would have something to take home," she confessed and handed, Marilyn the bag.

"Cookies, cookies, yea!" Reggie screamed and jumped up and down "I want one, I want one."

"Aunt Bea wants us to take them home, Reggie. We are going to sit down with glasses of cold milk and enjoy them while we think about our trip to Aunt Bea's house."

"Wait, wait," she pleaded as he tried to open the container. Opening the container she warned him, "Get only one."

"This is a big cookie!"

"Yes, Aunt Bea bakes the best cookies."

"It's g-o-o-d!"

Aunt Bea couldn't help noticing the look of despair on Ben's face, as he, without a word, turned and walked around to the back of the house. Marilyn hadn't even noticed. She was laughing and listening to Reggie explain how to make teacakes.

Aunt Bea followed Ben into the backyard. She found him sitting on the steps with his head down.

"Want a cookie?"

He looked up with a look that said it all.

"S-o-r-r-y, bad joke," she apologized.

She sat there for a moment and tried to find the right words to say what she had wanted to say since they had gotten there two days earlier.

"Ben, when you and Marilyn were married you all made the cutest couple I've ever seen. The chemistry between the two of you was so real. It was a joy to be around you. I saw a hint of that yesterday when Sarah took the kids to the movies."

Ben sat and stared down at the steps.

Aunt Bea continued, "Do you love your child?" He gave her a look that made her say, "Sorry, stupid question. I guess what I mean is . . ." She didn't know how to say what she was feeling. She made another attempt. "What I mean is, discipline is just as big a part of showing love as hugs and kisses."

"I love my wife and my son, Aunt Bea. It's frustrating watching how she lets him get away with everything. It's like . . . it's like she can't say no to him."

"Watching? What do you mean watching?" She looked him straight in the eye.

Ben tried to explain, "I try to avoid arguing, Aunt Bea."

"You were brought up in church. You know your role in the family," she reminded him.

"Are you still in church? Do you read your Bible? Is Marilyn saved?" Aunt Bea interrogated.

"Marilyn believes in God. She just doesn't think it takes all of that. She believes you can study and pray at home."

"Well, do you?"

"Huh?"

"Well, do you pray and study at home?" she asked with the tone that demanded an answer.

Reluctantly, he shook his head, no.

"A lot of parents don't realize, until it's too late, that children need spankings every now and then. A child can't grow up to be a mature and sensitive individual with only hugs and kisses anymore than a crop can be productive with only sunshine."

"I know that, but try telling that to Marilyn," he challenged. "Most of our fights, probably all of them, involve Reggie." With a heavy heart he confessed, "If something doesn't change and soon . . . well, I just don't know. I mean, it's something every single day. Like for example, on our way down Friday, Marilyn had packed Reggie a traveling kit."

He stood up, shook his head and continued "She had put some of his favorite books and toys in a bag along with coloring books and crayons. He had a box of brand new crayons with every color there is."

He walked back over to the steps and sat down. He hesitated for a moment. "I went to the mall to pick up a black jacket I saw in the sales ad. I decided to get Reggie some of his favorite jelly beans and a little something for Marilyn. She always brings me something back when she goes shopping. Anyway, she has always loved bright red lipstick. I picked up her favorite color and some cologne."

"Marilyn always puts her purse on the floor of the back seat while traveling, and when we stopped at the rest stop she reached for her purse, only to find Reggie coloring with her new lipstick. I wanted to tan his behind. Marilyn said it was only lipstick and that I was overreacting. She even insisted on giving me the money for it."

"Aunt Bea, it wasn't about the lipstick or the money. The fact is that Reggie should not have gone into his mother's purse. He is growing up

without boundaries. It's scary how she tries to justify everything he does. Let me give you another example."

He went on to tell her what had happened two weeks earlier. The weekend had started out beautifully. They had taken Reggie to a Disney movie.

Surprisingly, they enjoyed it just as much as he did.

That Sunday Marilyn had fixed Ben's favorite dinner: fried thin steaks, smothered with green pepper and onions, Crowder peas and okra, and corn muffins. She had also baked him an upside-down pineapple cake.

After dinner, they played Old Maid with Reggie and had really enjoyed a nice quiet evening. At bedtime Reggie asked his mom for a pop. Ben told him no and reminded him that he had one with his meal and there would be no liquids after seven. Reggie went to bed crying. A half of an hour later Ben went to tuck him in and there on the night stand was a half of can of pop. He felt the can. It was still cold. Marilyn had given it to him.

Aunt Bea gave him a hug and reminded him, "You are the head of your family. It requires making tough decisions. They may not always be pleasant ones but they have to be made and stuck to."

Ben tried to talk to Marilyn several times on the drive back when Reggie was asleep. Each time she managed to change the subject without addressing the real issues. Frustrated he tried to forget the whole incident, but he couldn't. It lingered in the back of his mind.

Chapter Ten

Two weeks later, lying on his back with his hands under his head, Ben played back the previous evening.

Reggie had refused to eat his peas and carrots; he wanted to eat a hot dog instead. No amount of coaxing could get him to change his mind. He refused. As any parent, it grieved Ben that he had to take a strong stand. But he knew he had to take it. Reggie was sent to bed without dinner. Not only did Reggie whine, but it also created friction between him and Marilyn.

Ben didn't sleep well. Had he been too hard on Reggie? Did he spend more time being the disciplinarian than he did being the loving father? Hearing the television he knew Reggie was up. He decided to make his son a special breakfast. He would also use the occasion to have a father and son talk.

He crawled out of bed slowly as not to disturb Marilyn, Frank reached over and turned the alarm off. He looked back at the bed as the floor squeaked under his feet. He stopped as she turned over. She adjusted the pillow under her head and was snoring softly in seconds.

He yawned and pushed open the bedroom door as he wiped sleep from his eyes, he looked down on the floor as something crumbled under his feet. Looking down he couldn't believe his eyes, a trail of cereal lead from the kitchen to the living room.

Furiously he followed the trail into the living room and became angrier with each step. He gasped as he stood in the living room doorway. There sat Reggie in the middle of the floor eating his cereal while watching cartoons. The table was covered with puddles of milk and cereal.

"R-e-g-i-n-a-l-d R-e-e-d!" His father shouted.

Seeing his father's face told Reggie he was in big trouble. He jumped up with panic on his face causing the bowl in his lap to make an even greater mess. Gritting his teeth, Ben said asked, "How many times have we told you to eat in the kitchen, young man?" Reggie stood staring as his eyes watched the hallway, waiting and wanting his mom to rescue him.

"I want this mess cleaned up, now!"

Benjamin sat down on the love seat as he felt his head begin to pound. He remembered what a supervisor had told them in a safety meeting about stress. He had informed them that one should, at the moment they start feeling tense, count to ten. He said count further if needed. Ben knew if ever there was a day to practice it—today was that day. He closed his eyes and began counting.

"One, two, three . . . ."

Marilyn rushed into the room tying her belt. Her mouth dropped. Reggie was busy trying to clean up the mess. The truth was he was only making it worse as he spread the soggy cereal over the floor with a towel.

Ben was quietly sitting on the love seat. His elbow was propped on the arm of the seat. He rested his face in his hand. The veins of his neck protruded as he slowly continued to count. "Ten, and eleven."

Her first impulse was to clean up the mess, but one look at Ben told her the floor could wait.

"Ben, are you okay?" She asked in a loving, caring voice. She sat down beside him wanting desperately to hear him say yes, knowing that he wasn't. She sat helplessly, longing to find some words to comfort him.

She motioned for Reggie to leave the room. With relief written on his face Reggie hurriedly left the room, returning only once to pick up *his bowl and spoon. She listened as he dropped them in the sink and closed his bedroom door.*

"Thirty eight, thirty nine," he continued.

"Ben."

He raised his hand as if to stop her.

"I'm okay. Seriously, I'm fine," he said out loud to convince himself as much as her. As he sat back on the couch there was a crunching sound. He felt between the cushions. He shook his head in disbelief as he held up a balled up napkin. He held it away from him and opened it cautiously. He wasn't sure what he would find.

Dried up lima beans.

Marilyn looked on. Ben shook his head. It had been about three weeks since they had lima beans for dinner. It was a wonder that they didn't have bugs and ants. Marilyn had caught Reggie balling up food in the napkins and paper towels before. They thought that he had stopped.

Ben looked up to see that Reggie had eased back into the living room and was sitting on the floor watching cartoons as though nothing had happened.

Bewildered, he looked at Marilyn. She shrugged her shoulders.

"We need to have a long talk," he said and pointed toward the kitchen.

"We can talk here," she patted the couch.

"I don't want him to hear."

"He's into his cartoons," she assured him.

Ben raised his finger as if to say, watch this.

"Marilyn, do you want some ice-cream?" he asked in a low voice.

"I want some, I want some," Reggie sang as he rushed to his mom grinning with anticipation.

One after another Marilyn started recalling incidents that should have been taken more serious.

One year, during the first two weeks of October, the temperature had dropped into the fifties. Anticipating an early winter, Marilyn put away all of their summer clothes. After she brought out their winter things she realized that Reggie had outgrown both of his winter coats. With winter fast approaching she would have to buy him another one soon.

Marilyn asked Ben to take Reggie to Lincoln Mall after she saw the promo about the Sesame Street characters being there on the last Saturday in October. He agreed with one condition. She would have to come along.

They normally parked in the back lot. It was the closest to the auto department. No matter how often they went, there was always something Ben had to get for the car. Some things were needs and some were just wants.

As they left the auto department, Ben smelled the popcorn and told Reggie that they would get some on their way out of the store. Reggie said okay as he scurried along ahead of them. Passing by two small boys with popcorn Reggie began to whine about the popcorn. Ben patiently reminded him that they would get some as soon as they got his coat and saw the Sesame Street characters.

Reggie literally fell out in the floor. As quickly as he hit the floor Ben was spanking his behind. One, two, three, four licks. Quickly, he snatched him up off the floor.

"Now you straighten up your face, right now!" Ben demanded. Slowly Reggie brought his sniffles to a halt as Marilyn looked on in total disbelief. She was furious. He was a child. All children had tantrums.

"Ben, I think you are overreacting. He's only a child," she said in a stern tone as passerbys looked on. Reggie rushed to his mother, recognizing that she was on his side.

Ben threw his hands up in the air, shook his head, and turned toward Marilyn. He ran his hand through his hair. As much as he possibly could, he took a deep breath and in a very calm voice he spoke.

"I need some air; when you finish, I'll be in the car."

Without waiting for a response, he turned and headed toward the exit door.

"Bennnnnnn!" she called loudly after him. He never broke his stride.

"Mommie, can we get some popcorn now, pleeeaaasssee?" Reggie asked as he swung Marilyn's arm back and forth.

"Sure, baby," she said softly as she wondered about Ben. Lately they had been arguing over the smallest things. Once again, Reggie was in the middle of it.

She also thought that maybe he was having some problems on the job. His patience was very short these days. He made an issue out of everything. He had stormed out of the house two weeks earlier when she had allowed Reggie to stay up until midnight. She didn't see the harm; after all, there was no school the next day.

A couple of weeks earlier, they had an argument after he had found out that the reason she had stayed home from church was not because Reggie wasn't feeling well. She stayed because Reggie said he didn't want to go to church every Sunday. In her defense, she said that forcing him to go every Sunday might cause him to grow up hating church.

Maybe, she wondered, this is the seven-year itch everybody talks about. Whatever it was she knew they were going to have to sit down and talk as soon as Reggie was in bed tonight.

"Come on, Mommie, the popcorn is over there."

"I'm coming," she whispered over her shoulder as she looked toward the exit.

"That's him. That's the one officer!" Ben heard someone shout behind him. He didn't have the slightest curiosity about what was happening behind him. He was more concerned about his marriage. It was obvious to everybody except Marilyn that Reggie had her wrapped around his little finger.

"Excuse me sir, may I speak with you for a moment?"

The voice was so close he turned to see what the commotion was. An overweight police officer walked quickly toward him, as an elderly women tried to keep pace.

"That's him," cried the elderly woman, nearly out of breath, as she wagged her finger and pointed at Ben who looked dumbfounded. The officer explained.

"Sir, a complaint has been made that you were beating your child at the other end of the corridor," he announced as he waited for Ben to either deny it or explain.

Ben looked immediately at the elderly woman. She stood with her head high, proud to have done her civic duty. She looked about sixty-five or seventy. She wore a loud flowery dress that looked like it would make a great bed comforter. Plastic bracelets encircled her wrists. Her hair was a bluish black with about a half-inch of white roots. Her eyebrows had been drawn on and were slightly crooked.

"Sir," said the officer getting Ben's attention.

"No, I didn't beat my child. I spanked my child." he corrected as he glared at the woman.

She stepped behind the officer and nervously twirled a string of red beads. The string broke which sent them falling to the floor. One by one they made a soft tapping sound as they hit the floor and bounced across the corridor in every direction. She hurriedly picked them up.

Feeling the tension brewing, the officer dismissed the elderly lady with, "Thank you ma'am. I appreciate your help."

She smiled proudly. "Just doing my duty," *she responded. She made no attempt to leave. He tipped his hat as if to say goodbye.*

She smiled sheepishly, turned and reluctantly walked off. She made several glances over her shoulder. They watched her disappear around the corner.

"Mr.?"

"Reed. Ben Reed."

"Mr. Reed, I have to investigate each accusation, no matter how petty it may seem." *He took a small notepad out of his back pocket and began to write.*

After writing only two or three words he tore the sheet out. It was the last sheet.

Noticing a trash receptacle a couple of feet away, he walked over and disposed of the empty pad. He folded the sheet of paper. He put it in his shirt pocket.

"Mr. Reed. I was patrolling the outside when you and your family arrived a short while ago. I saw you all get out of the car. You were driving a dark green Grand Prix. It was an eighty-eight." *The officer smiled as he gave the details.*

Ben was puzzled. It showed on his face.

The officer explained. "Oh, I remember because I just traded my car two weeks ago. I was sure that it was my car until I saw your interior. Mine was leather. Your's cloth."

Ben wondered where he was going with this.

"Mr. Reed, I saw the way you interacted with your wife and child. I saw how you played with him and how loving you were toward your wife. I must admit, a little envy tugged at my heart as I watched you all interact."

"I've been a officer for twenty-seven years," he added proudly. "I'm a good judge of character and I'm convinced that if you spanked your child it was warranted."

He continued, "I'm an officer of the law, Mr. Reed but I'm also a deacon. As an officer of the law I have to give it to you the way it is on the book, but as a deacon I have to give it to you the way it is in THE BOOK."

"Are you a Christian, Mr. Reed?"

Feeling guilty, Ben confessed, "Yes, I am but I haven't been attending church the way I know I should."

"No, I don't mean do you go to church. I mean are you a Christian?"

Ben looked confused. "I don't know what you mean."

The officer smiled. "One is about religion. One is about relationship."

"Take your wife. You don't just know about her. You live together. You fellowship. She communicates to you, and you communicate to her. That's relationship. That's what God wants you to have with Him."

Ben nodded.

"Mr. Reed, I'm going to give it to you straight up. With the stuff our kids are exposed to these days if . . ."

Crash!

Startled they both turned to see the trash receptacle lid fall to the floor. The elderly woman, face flushed with embarrassment, scrambled to pick it up. Her eavesdropping had been exposed. Her hands shook as she hurriedly replaced the lid. Not daring to look in their direction, she hurried off.

They looked at each other moments before they burst out in sheer laughter. The officer regained his composure and continued, "On a serious note. When I was a child, parents didn't have to fear the law when it came to raising their children. They nurtured them with love, clothes, food, and shelter and in return they expected the utmost respect. They knew that discipline was as much a part of parenting as love."

"What the law doesn't tell parents is that when they do their job early, less than likely I'll have to do mine later." Looking in the direction of the lady he added, "I'm sure she meant well, but I'll be willing to bet that the closest she's ever come to parenting is caring for a cat or a bird."

Ben smiled.

"Mr. Reed. I've raised three kids. Anyone who has ever raised a child knows that they are born with a rebellious nature. It's our responsibility to shape it while it's like a young twig. If we bend the twig while it is young, it will grow in the bent position. If we wait 'til the twig is grown and try to bend it, the twig will snap."

"In the book of Proverbs it tells us about parenting. It tells you that rebellion is born in a child and it has to be dealt with. It also tells us that if we spank them they are not going to die."

"I hope you are listening to me. In the times we are living, if you try to raise your child the way God wants you to, you are going to be

89

criticized, condemned, and maybe even jailed. It's going to come down to what's more important to you, doing the right thing or doing what's politically correct. In these times you are going to find out how strong your faith is."

He stretched out his hand and gripped Ben's firmly. Benjamin sensed he wanted to say more. Smiling he gave him a slap on the shoulder. He raised his hand.

"Remember."

Someone summoned him on his walkie-talkie and within seconds, with a wave of his hand, he was gone.

Chapter Eleven

Ben *needed fresh air and* headed for the exit. He had to have some fresh air. He usually complained about how much time it took her to shop, but not today. He needed time to be alone to think.

Reggie and Marilyn always played a game called *Same Kind*. The first to find a car like theirs: same model and color would be the winner. Today, Reggie felt the tension. He sat quietly on the seat reading one of his books as they left the parking lot.

Ben took the long route home. Marilyn was sure he took it to delay getting home. However, it pleased her because they would pass one of her favorite sights. It was a beautiful white farmhouse with a sprawling rich green lawn. It sat about half a city block off the expressway. It was nestled between large maple trees.

Year around, children could usually be seen playing in the yard. Sometimes they would be making snowmen or playing football in the winter or jumping rope or making giant bubbles in the summer. A young woman was often cutting or chopping around the flowers while a young man was often riding a mower.

The house is just ahead, thought Marilyn, recognizing the giant billboard. Today, of all days, while feeling so distant from her husband she needed to feel that sense of joy, happiness and love. She longed for that sense of family, that feeling of warmth. However, to her surprise the house looked abandoned and the lawn in dire need of mowing. There was no sign of life. How *coincidental*.

A few weeks later while driving home, Ben flipped on the turn signal *and noticed* the traffic was unusually heavy as he proceeded to maneuver to the right. His exit was next—less than a quarter of a mile away. He threw his hand up in gratitude as the driver slowed down and allowed him to cross over as he approached the exit.

"Now, that's scary," whispered Ben. He had driven the entire route and didn't remember passing some of the landmarks along the way. It was if his car was on automatic pilot.

Out of the corner of his eye the driver's frantic waving caught Ben's attention. Shaking his head Ben smiled with recognition and shook his head. The driver motioned for Ben to pull over. It was T.J., a friend from high school. Both had been members of the football and track teams. *T.J. had earned a scholarship to a great school on the West Coast and was viewed as having the potential to play professional football.* He had been pro material winning a scholarship to a great school on the West-Coast. The last thing Ben had heard was that he had injured his knee during practice and wasn't able to play.

The street was a snow route with no parking when there was three inches or more of snow. There were about six inches on the ground. With nowhere nearby to park Ben pulled over and cut off the engine. He would only be a moment and the car wouldn't be left unattended.

"Mr. T.J. Brown. Man, it's good to see you! What has it been thirteen, fourteen years?" he asked, shaking his hand.

"Something like that," he responded, grinning sheepishly.

Ben shook his hand *and gave* him a bear hug. "It's good to see you. I was sorry to hear about your injury. Man, you were good."

"Correc-t-i-o-n. You were G-O-O-D. I was g-r-e-a-t!"

Ben laughed *and remembered* how *T.J.* always kept the team laughing and in good spirit. He didn't have a prideful bone in his body—just a funny bone. He kept the morale up whether they were winning or losing.

"Yeah, I have to admit, you're right," Ben confessed.

"Seriously, how have you been? Happily married? Children?"

"Yes." Not happy lately, Ben thought. "One son," he added, turning up the collar on his wool coat.

"That's great. As for me, I'm not married yet, but there's a young lady who's getting tired of waiting. She's great. I guess I'm just scared of making a commitment. You see so many of your friends relationships go bad that you just," he shrugged his shoulders. "I don't know."

"What are you doing now? Are you back in the city?" Ben asked. He was eager to change the subject.

"No. I'm still in L.A. My mom has been sick for a couple of weeks. She wanted all of us to come home for her birthday. I flew in this morning *and did a little shopping*. I'm helping her fix dinner this evening. As for the job I'm vice president of a small accounting office in L.A. It's small but growing. As a matter of fact we're always looking for good accountant. You could get your degree. If I remember correctly you were always good in math. If you are ever interested in relocating, saying good-bye to this cold weather, give me a call. It would be great for your wife and son. A lot of great schools." He *encouraged* as he pulled off his glove and reached into his inside coat pocket for a business card.

He opened his car door and grabbed his hat off the seat.

Ben noticed several beautifully wrapped boxes on the seat. Shivering T.J. confessed, "This is a great place to live, but I sure don't miss this part. Send in your resume. I'll take a look at it. Put it to my attention," he said scribbling something on the card.

Reading the card Ben shot back, "And if I remember correctly, when it came to math, you were good, I was g-r-e-a-t!!

93

T.J. raised his gloved hand high in the air and made two check marks: one to his left and one to his right.

"Score even. One to one."

They both laughed.

With not the slightest intention of using it, Ben put the card in his pocket. He thanked T.J. and promised to give him a call if he ever became tired of the long cold winters. They shook hands and promised to keep in touch.

One after another, Marilyn remembered episodes with Reggie that she had allowed to go unchecked.

"I need to get some batteries; I'll only be a moment," Ben said, as he pulled into the drugstore parking lot.

"Ahhh look, those big birds" cried Reggie excited.

"Yep, those are Sea G-u-l-l-s," pronounced Ben.

"Sea G-u-l-l-s," repeated Reggie.

"Sea Gulls," nodded Marilyn.

She lovingly touched the tip of his nose. He giggled and wiggled out of her reach.

"You guys need anything?" asked Ben unfastening his seat belt.

Reggie's mouth gasped opened as he took a deep breath, "I want . . ."

"We know what you want," Marilyn interjected.

"I want M & Ms and . . ."

"Reggie. You can have only one bag of candy" Ben said firmly.

"What's wrong, Lynn?" asked Ben seeing the puzzled look on her face.

"Nothing, it's just that I need to pick up something," Marilyn said, remembering the red circle on the calendar.

"What? I'll get it."

"No, I don't think so."

He recognized that tone.

"Yes, I think you better come with us," he laughed. She elbowed him in the side before taking his hand.

"What's so funny?" Reggie asked puzzled looking from one parent to the other for an explanation.

"What kind of candy did you say you want?" Ben asked Reggie avoiding the question.

Marilyn gave him a look. "Very, very clever."

*   *   *

Ben met Marilyn at the front of the store. "Did you find what you needed?" he ribbed.

"Yes, I did?" she replied cradling the small package in her arm.

"Where's Reggie?" she asked.

"I thought he was with you."

"He was, but . . ."

"Check the candy aisle while I check the toys. No need to panic," he reassured her.

Ben and one of the stock boys searched every aisle, meeting Marilyn at the front of the store. While the stock boy went to get the manager, as much as he possibly could, Ben tried to comfort her. Little did she know that his palms were beginning to sweat. On other occasions they would find him playing with the toys or looking at the candies. This time, Reggie was not in the store.

Ben avoided eye contact with Marilyn. She could read him like a book. The last thing he wanted was for her to see the fear that was invading his mind.

She wanted to run, but where?

He wanted to do something, but what?

She tried to stay calm to block out unpleasant possibilities, as news headlines flashed before her.

Looking to Ben for comfort she noticed his right arm stiff against his leg as he flexed his hand continually. It was a dead give away to the helplessness he was feeling.

Marilyn looked for a chair. She had to sit. Her heart was heavy.

"We found him!" shouted one of the workers coming in the front door.

"He was outside playing with the seagulls." He added contrastingly. "He was having a ball."

Marilyn rushed over to Reggie as he stood looking perplexed, wondering what all the fuss was about.

"Baby." She dropped down on her knees before him and hugged him as if she never wanted to let him go.

Relieved that he was safe, she shook him. "You scared Mommy and Daddy. Don't you ever wander off like that again, you hear?"

"I'm sorry, mommy," he sang in his sweet little voice as he started to cry.

Marilyn smiled. Standing up she shook the employee's hand and thanked him.

"Let's get those M & Ms," she announced dabbing at her eyes.

Chapter Twelve

After an unusually hard day at work, Ben had picked up Chinese takeout for dinner. As he poured some fried rice into a bowl he thought of Marilyn. Fried rice and egg rolls were her favorite.

As Ben stirred the rice, his thoughts went back to the night he left.

Ben carefully folded several white shirts and dark pants and placed them in the bottom of the duffel bag. He threw some socks, t-shirts and briefs on top. He recalled T.J. saying the weather was in the low 80's as he pulled out his bottom drawers. It felt strange packing summer clothes with the weather in the low 40's. He selected two pair of walking shorts Marilyn had bought him for his birthday. Although he often wore them around the house, he never ventured out in them. The memories of being teased as a teen about his skinny, knotty knees were imbedded in his mind. He rolled up the shorts and placed them in the corner of his bag. Traveling light has its drawbacks, he thought as he struggled to zip the bag.

He took his checkbook off the closet shelf and examined it for a moment before laying it on the night stand. He turned off the light. As he turned around, the tip of his bag knocked a book off the night stand. In the dark he braced for the inevitable. Nothing, not even a ruffling of covers, just a light snore filled the room. Ben was a light sleeper; Marilyn was just the opposite. He had often teased that someone could move her and the bed out onto the street, and she wouldn't know it until the alarm sounded.

The floor squeaked as he crossed the room. He sat his bag in the hallway. He pulled an envelope from his back pocket as he walked back across the room. Picking the book off the floor he laid it on the night stand. As it was almost mornings, her pillow was on the floor. He placed it gently above her head.

He had called T.J. two days earlier. Living arrangements had been made, the flight had been booked, and his bag was now packed. As he stood watching Marilyn sleep, it was hard to believe that his marriage was over. Reggie's antics were usually at the center of their arguments. However, lately Ben had noticed they were arguing over trivial things.

As he tucked the comforter around her shoulders there was a strong desire to cradle her in his arms. She turned over as she rubbed her eyes with the back of her hand. He stood still, not wanting to wake her. The last thing he wanted at this point was a confrontation. His heart was already hurting. He didn't think it was possible, but the last few months she had become even more beautiful. She had a glow. He recalled his days as a child. He would lie in bed at night fearful of what might happen, pleading with God to stop his parents from arguing. Even though he loved his mom and his dad, he secretly longed for his dad to leave just so there would be peace. Eventually, however, his parents outgrew their antics and became a happy couple.

Holding the letter in his hand, he struggled with whether to leave it or call her from the airport. Finally, he propped it between the book and the alarm clock. He picked up his bag and quietly closed the door. Halfway down the hall he suddenly stopped and turned back. Quietly he turned the knob, and pushed the door ajar. Something about the closed door gave him a feeling of finality. He wasn't sure that was what he wanted. He just knew they needed time and space. What was once their home was now just a house. There was no peace.

Ben slowly pushed open Reggie's door. The light from the hall flooded the room. The sheets were turned back, but the bed was empty. There at the foot of the bed was his son asleep on the floor in a pile of coloring books, crayons and action figures. Reggie's arms wrapped around his dad's neck as Ben picked him up. A pain tugged at Ben's heart as he realized that by the time his son woke up that morning, he would be in California.

After tucking him in Ben watched as his son slept peacefully. He loved his son and his wife, and he was sure they loved him. He didn't understand it, but he was just as sure that he had to go. Crayons crunched under his feet as he made his way out the room. He was reminded of a weekend he had kept Reggie alone.

Reggie was four when Aunt Liz had a terrible bout with the flu and was in bed the weekend. Uncle Robert was out of town and Marilyn volunteered to stay with her from Friday afternoon until Uncle Robert returned on Sunday evening. Ben and Reggie had a great time. They made pallets on the living room and colored and ate hotdogs that Friday evening. They went to the park that Saturday and flew a kite until it became tangled in a tree. That Sunday they saw a Disney movie and ate a bucket of popcorn. The father and son laughed and had a great time the entire weekend.

Both days they were up at seven and in bed by eight. Not once did Ben have to raise his voice or repeat himself. They both had the time of their life just father and son. However the moment Marilyn returned that Sunday, Reggie was whining and crying about going to bed at nine. He didn't want to take his bath until his mom promised to take him to McDonald's the next day.

Ben stopped and turned at the door. Reggie was sleeping soundly. He looked so innocent and helpless. Ben knew his son and wife needed him. But he also knew he had to find what he needed—whatever that was.

At that very same time over 2,000 miles away Marilyn is reliving that very same day.

Marilyn remembered awaking to the loud plopping sound of rain on the windowsill. She realized the temperature had dropped as she threw the *comforter back and slipped into her slippers. After her morning routine of yawns and stretches, she pulled her robe from the bedpost and flipped the lamp switch. Stuck between the book and the alarm clock was an envelope in Ben's handwriting. It was addressed to her. A feeling of uneasiness came over her instantly. Ben wasn't a writer. He had often teased saying he hadn't written a letter since he found out as a child that there was no Santa Claus. As she held the envelope her body began to shake with anxiety.*

She read the letter over and over again. Still it didn't register. Her mind simply wouldn't let her go there. If this was his idea of a joke, it wasn't funny. If he was trying to get her attention, well, finally he had it. She slumped down to the floor.

She read on. "I had to do it this way."

A chill swept over the room.

Loneliness filled her chest.

An ache tugged at her heart.

With her head down she sat clutching her knees. She wondered how she would make it through the day. Getting through the ordeal was too much to dare ponder. The pouring rain and the crackling sound of thunder drowned out her sobs.

After sitting on the floor for hours, a distraught Marilyn put a cold compress to her tight, bloodshot eyes. As soon as the sun came up she called Nikki. Giving no advice Nikki assured her that everything would be fine. She was on her way to work but would call on her first break. She encouraged Marilyn to call Uncle Robert and Aunt Liz before breaking the news to Reggie. Marilyn had promised.

Marilyn was hoping that Aunt Liz would answer the phone. Her prayer was answered. They were in the middle of breakfast but promised to come as soon as possible. Aunt Liz sensed the urgency in her voice.

Marilyn watched out of the window. She didn't want the doorbell to wake Reggie. In less than an hour they pulled in front of the house. Marilyn opened the door before Uncle Robert could press the bell. Aunt Liz pushed past Uncle Robert. Marilyn ran straight into Aunt Liz's waiting arms.

She shared with them bits and pieces from the letter. Oblivious to Marilyn, neither showed any sign of surprise. They exchanged several glances as she spoke. This certainly wasn't the right time to say it. There may never be a right time. One thing for sure, Aunt Liz couldn't help thinking, "I told you so."

The next few weeks were awful. Reggie was constantly whining and asking for his dad. She didn't know what to tell him. How do you tell a seven year-old that Daddy won't be coming home? On top of that Marilyn was sick practically every day. She wasn't sure whether or not it was from stress or the flu. Nothing would stay on her stomach. At times she couldn't get out of bed, she'd ask Nikki to come over before she went to work.

On several occasions while talking to Nikki on the phone, during the breakfast hours, Marilyn had to rush to the bathroom. She tried to assure her friend that the nausea was caused by a flu bug, but Nikki wasn't convinced. Nikki suggested that maybe she should see a gynecologist. She reminded her that pregnancy couldn't be ruled out. Marilyn continued insisting that it was a touch of stomach flu and nothing more. Two weeks later as symptoms persisted, Marilyn reluctantly agreed, insisting that Nikki go with her for support.

Without an appointment her wait was more than an hour to see her gynecologist. However, in just ten minutes of changing into her paper gown, Marilyn walked out fully dressed looking oblivious to everything. Her eyes were fixed straight ahead. With the exception of a cane she could have easily been mistaken for a blind person. She walked across the waiting room and without a word sat on the couch beside Nikki.

"The rabbit died."

Within seconds Marilyn burst into tears. Nikki cried too as she wondered how to get in touch with Ben. A part of Marilyn was excited about the baby; hopefully, it would be a girl. Ben had wanted their next child to be a girl. Immediately sadness and fear of raising two children without their father welled up within her and sent her rushing down the hall to the bathroom.

On the drive home it was unusually quiet. Usually their drives would be filled with laughter and chatter as they cut each other off with funny stories mostly about work. Today was different. The ride was too quiet, Nikki thought, as she reached for the radio knob. Nikki hated city driving, but had insisted on driving back knowing that Marilyn's mind wouldn't be on the road. She wanted to say something to get her mind off what the doctor had just said, but didn't know what. So she kept silent.

"Are you hungry, shall we grab a bite to eat?" Nikki asked breaking the silence. No response. "Earth to Mars, Earth to Mars." It was what they always said when the other one wasn't paying attention. Taking her right hand off the steering wheel she wiggled her fingers up and down in front of Marilyn. "Is anybody home?" Nikki would readily understand that Marilyn was not in a playful mood. This comes across as insensitivity.

"Sorry, what were you saying?" she forced a smile.

"Should we stop for a bite to eat? I'm a little hungry, and I know you must be also. After all, you are eating for . . ." She caught herself before she said two. Real smart Nikki she said to herself. You and your big mouth did it again.

"Sorry, my big mouth went before my brain, AGAIN."

"It's okay, really. I am eating for two now. The sooner I get used to it the better it'll be for both of us," she said, as she rubbed her flat stomach as she fought back tears.

"Man, I had better stop for gas before we have to push this car," Nikki said, as she noticed the gas hand dangle close to E.

"Turn at the next light."

"Right or left?" asked Nikki as she neared the intersection.

"Right, no, no, I mean left!" shouted Marilyn holding out her left hand.

"Okay, now that we have learned our left from our right, tomorrow we will work on tying our shoes," Nikki teased.

As Nikki pulled into the station, a shiny, black, stretch limousine pulled alongside of her leaving very little room for her to get out. Nikki gasped with a look of, "Can you believe this?" She squeezed out of the car, trying not to scratch the limousine with her door.

The chauffeur, dressed in black from head to toe, stepped out of the car. Hurriedly, he opened the side door. A beautiful young woman, in her early twenties, with flawless skin, dressed in evening attire with lots of glittery jewelry hurriedly exited the car and disappeared into the station. In a moment she returned followed by another young woman laughing. As the limo pulled off, the other young lady waved to Nikki as she placed the nozzle in the tank.

Pointing to the exiting limo, "When it comes to some things even the rich are on the same level with us." Nikki was confused until she explained, "The bathroom. When nature calls we all have to ANSWER."

"I know that's right," chuckled Nikki as she opened the car door.

Putting the key in the ignition she noticed Marilyn's head back on the seat facing the window. She'd never seen her friend so sad. She was the one that was always upbeat and perky. With her eyes closed Marilyn spoke, "It would be so good to just lay down and sleep."

Silence.

Marilyn opened her eyes to find Nikki with the oddest expression on her face.

"Ah, no girl, don't be crazy," she assured Nikki when it dawned on her what she was thinking. "No matter how hard life is, it's always worth living. Always! I meant sleep as in e-i-g-h-t hours. Lately everything I eat and drink gives me heartburn. I'm up most of the night and I—I miss Ben. I miss him so much."

With a sigh of relief Nikki promised, "I'm here and you can call me anytime no matter how late." Laughing she added, "After all, there have been plenty of nights you kept me from drowning my sorrows in a half gallon of butter pecan. Why, I would probably be weighing fifty pounds more if it wasn't for your support."

Chapter Thirteen

Ben had been in Los Angeles 6 years. The pain was just as real as it was the first day he thought as he slumped down on the stool. Unfolding his paper, he waved to get the waitress' attention.

"Be there in a minute!" she yelled. Obviously annoyed at being interrupted, she took her time. She wiped off the counter, changed the coffee filter, and stacked the cups in the rack. Finally she came to the end of the counter. If she was trying to needle him she failed. He hadn't even realized how much time she had taken. He was totally focused on the sports section.

"What can I do for you?" she growled. The first thing that jumped in his mind was to suggest she start by being polite. Instead in his most pleasant cheerful voice he gave his order.

"Large coffee, cream and sugar, please," He stated without looking up. With a pen in hand she waited.

"Is that all?" she asked with contempt, thumping her pad with the pen.

"Yes, thank you," he replied as he looked up from his paper. Ignoring her look of disdain, he folded his paper in half and continued to read. His grandmother had always advised him to never allow other to bring him down to their level.

"What happened? Little Lady didn't make your breakfast this morning?"

He looked up from his paper to see an attractive, casually-dressed young lady about his age. She wore jeans and a tank top. He smiled. She picked up his jacket and was about to lay it aside.

"I'll take that, thank you," he said moving his jacket.

She took the stool and put her purse and cell phone on the counter in front of her. The waitress returned and placed a large cup of coffee, two creams and four sugars in front of him. She looked from the woman to him. With a roll of her eyes, she laid his check down and walked off.

Noticing, the woman replied, "Maybe she needs that cup of coffee more than you."

He was thinking the same thing. He smiled.

Her phone rung.

"Excuse me," she said politely. She chatted briefly and hung up.

"How about breakfast?" She added, "On me, of course."

"Thanks," he replied standing to his feet. "But no thanks," he added taking a big gulp.

"Are you sure?" she asked gently touching his arm. "I hate eating alone."

He turned over his bill. Large coffee: $1.05.

He pulled several crumbled dollars from his pocket. He laid two beside the unused sugar, shoving the other one back in his pocket. The waitress stood to the side, with her arms folded, and observed the scene. He smiled politely.

He pulled the dollar from his pocket and added it to the other two. Kill her with kindness.

"Sorry, I'm married," he announced, zipping up his jacket.

She smiled and threw up her hands, "I don't mind."

Picking up his paper he replied, "But I do."

Chapter Fourteen

Ben had arrived in California with only a duffle bag and a C D player, 6 years later, he didn't own much more. He assured him that his apartment was roomy enough for the both of them. Having arrived that Saturday afternoon, Ben was able to take care of the paperwork Monday and start to work that Tuesday. It wasn't the job that he had anticipated but the pay was good. The work was strenuous and the hours were long, leaving little time for anything else. That was the way he wanted it. Faithfully, on the first of each month he sent Marilyn money. He always sent a money order with no return address less lest she return it.

Several times he wrote notes only to tear them up. What would he say? How are you? I miss you?

As he sat across from Carol (she hadn't given a last name) he played with his napkin. He couldn't remember the last time he had dined with a woman other than Marilyn. It had been years. He studied her face as she read the menu. It didn't reveal anything other than the fact she was beautiful, naturally beautiful. He saw no make-up. She seemed very confident. "I guess you'd have to say she's a little assertive," he thought. After all she was at his table even though he didn't want the company.

He had declined an invitation to have dinner with T.J. and his fiancé. Without being rude he had expressed the desire to be alone.

Wanting a nice quiet evening alone, he had purposely chosen a small table near the back. Carol, seated at a table nearby, asked if she could join him. She confided that her date had stood her up, and that she hated eating alone. His mind was shouting, "No, No, No!" But not wanting to be rude he followed his heart and said, "Sure."

With his fingers, he did drum rolls on the table to make sure she saw his wedding band. He wanted it to be clear the only thing they would be sharing was a table. He hoped she wasn't expecting him to keep the conversation flowing. If so, she was sadly mistaken.

As he looked at the menu he remembered the last time he had gone out to dinner with Marilyn. It was her birthday and he had wanted to have a nice quiet evening with her. Things hadn't been going well between them lately, and he'd wanted to have a fresh start. Uncle Robert and Aunt Liz were out of town and Nikki had to work. Unable to get a sitter on short notice, they had taken Reggie. Ben ordered Marilyn's favorite, Alfredo Fettuccini, for the two of them, and for Reggie, who didn't like cheese, he ordered a burger with fries. Reggie began to whine and protest because he wanted what they were having. Ben patiently explained to Reggie that their food had lots of cheese. The waitress, with pen in hand, stood by waiting patiently. Her money was on the child. She'd seen it happen too many times before.

"That will be all," Ben assured her, folding the menu. Unconvinced, she nodded and left.

"I do like cheese," Reggie insisted.

Marilyn cut in. "Reggie, you are going to have French fries with ketchup. Mmmm, it's going to be good."

"I want chinnie fritos," he whined.

Not wanting to ruin the evening, Ben pretended to read the menu and allowed her to handle the situation. He hoped she would put her foot down, at least one time.

"Excuse me," called Marilyn getting their waitress's attention.

"I'd like to change our order, please. Make that three Alfredo Fettuccini, please.

"Sure, no problem," she replied, making a notation on her pad. Sticking her pen in her hair she mumbled under her breath, "One for the kid. Zero for the parents."

Determined to salvage some of the evening Ben tried to be as cheerful as possible. He shared some funny incidents with Marilyn about the job. They laughed and talked while waiting for their meal.

The waitress smiled as she sat Reggie's plate in front of him. She'd seen this scene played out so many times before. She hoped this one would have a different ending. Looking pleased, Reggie grabbed his fork. With his hand he carefully folded the noodles on his fork. The waitress slowly placed the other two plates on the table. Her eyes were on Reggie. She was hoping the parents would even the score. Not wanting to be obvious, the waitress busied herself at the table nearby. She arranged and rearranged condiments as she waited for the expected ending. The food fell off the fork again before it reached his mouth. Seemingly unaware, Ben and Marilyn were busy chatting. Patiently Reggie had folded it on his fork again, only this time he held it until it was in his mouth. He frowned. Leaning over his plate he allowed the food to fall from his mouth.

"Yuck," he said frowning. With the back of his hand he wiped the cheese from his mouth.

"You don't like it?" Ben asked as if he didn't know the answer.

Reggie shook his head.

"Drink your milk, you can have cereal when you get home."

"I want a hamburger."

Ben laid his fork down and wiped his mouth on his napkin. He'd had enough.

"Look young man . . . ," he said firmly.

Marilyn raised her arm to get getting the waitress's attention.

Again the waitress mumbled, "Two to zero, in favor of the kid."

Carol reached across the table, tapped Ben's hand with her menu.

"Looks like you were reliving some unhappy moments. Is everything okay?" she asked curiously.

"Sorry," he added, "Everything's fine." Having consented to sharing his table, he was beginning to think even that it was a bad idea. The last thing he was about to do was share any of his personal life with a total stranger.

Not only was she beautiful, but she was also well educated also. She had graduated from a small school out East, but had recently moved back to her divorced sister with her small children.

After giving his order, Ben excused himself, expressing a need to wash his hands. Actually, he was giving his ears a rest and minimizing the time they had to converse. He stood in the mirror combing his hair over and over, not trying to look attractive. He wanted to return only seconds before his dinner was served. Marilyn always tried to encourage him to not rush through his meals. It was a habit that he hadn't been able to break. Tonight, it would be a good thing.

Ben noticed a tall gray-haired man talking with Carol as he crossed the room. They were in deep conversation.

"Call me at seven," she called out as the gentleman walked away. He wondered what that was all about. He quickly dismissed it; after all she wasn't with him. Hopefully, she would be out of his life in the next ten or fifteen minutes. Ben's face dropped as he neared the table. The waitress had brought his Alfredo Fettuccini served with a golden, baked chicken breast. It looked delicious.

"This is my first time trying this. It's great, dig in," she instructed, cutting her chicken into bite size pieces. I don't think so, he thought. Call it paranoia if you like, but after seeing his classmates put salt in the sugar shaker in college, he never left his food unattended unless with family and friends. Carol was neither.

Pulling his chair from the table, he contemplated how he would avoid eating his meal. He was about to sit, when an elderly man dressed in street clothes walked up. Flashing a badge, he introduced himself.

"Officer Martin, third precinct. I need you to follow me, sir," he ordered in a low voice as not to disturb the patrons. He gave no information.

"What? There has to be some mistake," Ben insisted, pushing his chair under the table.

"No mistake, sir," he assured him. Carol looked on in sheer dismay.

"May I see your I.D., please?" Ben gave his license without hesitation. He began to feel uncomfortable as some of the patrons began to whisper.

The officer studied it for a moment. Without giving it back, in a quiet tone he instructed Ben to follow him. As they walked toward the door the officer asked Ben several questions, looking down as if to compare answers with his notes.

Once outside, the officer returned his license with a warning to be careful while visiting their city. He informed him that the young lady had a record of robbery. She was working with an older man medium build, salt and pepper hair, he description matched the man talking to her at the table. They had been under surveillance for the last few weeks.

The officer informed Ben that in the last two months several businessmen woke up finding themselves in strange places. The last thing they remembered was having dinner with her. One found himself in a nearby city. Needless to say, their valuables were missing. Whereas none suffered physical harm, all suffered financially, emotionally and embarrassingly. Because of their families not one would press charges.

Relieved, yet feeling somewhat naive Ben thanked the officer.

Before walking off, the officer gave Ben some advice, "free" as he put it.

"Remember, eating alone is not as bad as it seems. We sometimes think that a pretty face makes a meal taste better. Believe me, it can sometimes give you chronic indigestion. I know she looks like she's sweet, innocent like she wouldn't hurt a fly."

He shook his head.

"Cold. Callous. Nerves of steel."

"You know," he shook his head, "times are really changing. I used to give this lecture to women. Now more and more I'm giving it to men. Don't let loneliness make you vulnerable. I heard someone say—one is a whole number."

Ben wanted to explain that this wasn't the case. Sensing the officer had made up his mind, Ben thanked him. Still hungry, he headed home.

Marilyn picked up the phone to call Aunt Liz. After seeing Reggie, she just wanted to hold them tight. As she sat on the bed, she reflected back to the day she learned she was having twins.

It *was 10:16 a.m. For the first time, Marilyn was early for her doctor's appointment. Placing her jacket on the back of the chair she reached for a magazine. There was nothing interesting on the table. She slipped her shoes off and leaned back on the sofa. Her feet felt heavy.*

Looking down she wiggled her toes. In the last two weeks she had noticed her feet had begun to swell. Dr. White had assured her on the phone that it was just water retention. No reason to be alarmed. She hated waiting, especially at the doctor's office.

Unlike some offices, there was no television or soft music. She would suggest that they at least keep a selection of current ladies magazines. Feeling sleepy, she reached for a magazine on parenting.

She was turning the pages, but she wasn't interested in the magazine. Her attention was drawn to the couple at the opposite end of the room. The lady was about her age and the man was slightly older. She was rubbing her stomach while her head rested on his shoulder. Marilyn couldn't hear what he was saying, but she could tell that they were words of comfort. The woman looked relaxed as he stroked her head.

Marilyn looked down at her stomach. They were both about four months' pregnant, about the same age but with one big difference.

Marilyn was alone.

The love they had for each other could be felt as they talked quietly. They were oblivious to everything and everyone around them.

Envy began to sweep over Marilyn as she longed for Ben. He had always been so supportive and attentive during her pregnancy. She fought back tears knowing once they were unleashed they would be virtually impossible to stop.

"Marilyn?"

"Hi, is Mr. Reed with you today?"

"No, he's not!" she shot back. Immediately she regretted her words. They were spoken out of her pain.

"I'm sorry. It's just . . ."

"No need to apologize. I've had three children. I know how the hormones are," the nurse assured her.

She smiled, all the while wanting to say, it's not hormones this time, it's envy as she glanced at the couple. Before she could start having a pity party the nurse ushered her into the room to take her vitals and change into a gown. She raised her paper gown and rubbed her stomach. Her stomach growled. The nurse turned, smiled, and left the room. Marilyn wasn't embarrassed. She was too hungry to care. She reached for her purse. Hearing the doctor outside of the door she quickly bit off the candy bar. The door opened before she could swallow.

One look at him, and she knew he had seen her chewing. Now she'd have to hear a lecture about eating right or the weight she'd gained. Knowing that she had been busted, there was no need to hide it. There was only one thing to do now.

"Want a piece?"

He shook his head and took a seat. He jotted something in her folder.

No lecture.

No jokes.

She studied his face. Something was wrong.

Dr. White was in his early sixties. He had been her doctor when she was pregnant with Reggie. What she liked about him most was his ability to make her feel at ease. His sense of humor and genuine sense of concern made her comfortable. Something was wrong with this picture.

Wrapping the partly eaten candy bar, she pleaded,

"Alright, what's wrong?"

"Nothing," he replied searching for the right way to tell her.

He was making her nervous. Was the baby okay? Was something wrong with her blood work? What? What?

"No. Seriously," he replied, "Nothing's wrong, nothing's wrong."

Again he responded, "Everything's fine, everything's fine."

"I'm not being funny Dr. White, but you are beginning to annoy me. Not only are you not giving me any information but why in the world are you saying everything's . . . ."

He smiled as it finally sunk in.

"No, you don't mean . . . ."

He nodded. "Yes, twins. There's clearly two strong heartbeats."

For a moment she was in shock, then, she broke into laughter. She'd always wanted twins. Oh, daughters, she hoped. She could dress them in pretty bright colored dresses with ribbons and barrettes. Without warning the next minute she was crying hysterically. With a daughter of his own, Dr. White sympathized with her. He passed her a box of tissues as he listened patiently. She shared her fears of raising three children alone.

Marilyn had been a patient of Dr. White for years. He wasn't one to rush through visits. He was from the old school. He listened and got to know his patients. He knew Marilyn was stronger than she thought. Not only that, he was convinced that she could handle whatever hand life dealt her.

Chapter Fifteen

The moment he stepped aboard the plane, anxiety washed over him like a tidal wave along on the California shoreline. His heart began to palpitate. His palms were sticky. *He constantly wiped his sticky palms on his legs as he made his way to the counter.* He had planned to take the train the next time he went home. However, at his mother's urging, he was taking a plane. Mr. Saunders, his father's best friend, was hospitalized, and was asking for Ben.

Ben had made plans to return to Chicago several times, to try to reconcile with Marilyn. But, each time, the guilt of abandonment overruled, he didn't feel he deserved a second chance.

It had been six years since Ben left. For six long years he had buried himself in his work. Out side of the job he only socialized with a handful of people; *mostly T.J.'s friends.* His co-workers thought he was a strange character and that was fine. It kept them at a distance.

Lately, Ben had been doing a lot of reflecting on his life. On this flight he didn't need a seat by the window. On this trip he would be looking within. Although he could well afford first class, he opted for coach. One thing he had learned. When there's no peace in your heart, no place will be comfortable.

As the plane taxied down the runway he prayed. Like he had done so many times before, he asked the Lord to soften Marilyn heart and let her understand what he was feeling the day he left.

"Are you all right, Sir?" the flight attendant asked.

"I'm fine. Just a little queasy."

"Can I get you something?" He shook his head.

Negative. This queasiness wasn't from the flight, but the fear of returning home.

"Wait, let me get the phone," pleaded Marilyn as she crawled across the kitchen floor. Bianca followed desperately trying to untangle the comb from Marilyn's hair.

"Ma, I ain't finished," cried Ben Jr., *as he* screwed the top on the polish bottle.

"I know, just a minute," Marilyn promised as she picked up the receiver. She tapped Bianca on the shoulder and whispered, "Pass Mommy a tissue, please."

"Thank you, baby," whispered Marilyn, and dabbed the polish between her toes.

"Hi, Marilyn," said Nikki. "I was just wondering whether or not you want to go to the movies with us tomorrow night? Charlene saw that suspense thriller we were talking about last week. She said it's great!"

"Us, as in who?"

"Anthony and I are going. One of his cousins has moved here from Dallas. I thought maybe the four of us could go," she said trying hard to make it not sound like a blind date.

"Thanks, but I'll pass," she said.

"Marilyn, Ben has been gone six years. Are you planning to spend the rest of your life single? Are you going to wait on him forever?" Oh, no. She hadn't meant to go there.

"Marilyn, I'm sorry. I didn't mean . . ." Nikki apologized.

"I know you meant well, Nikki," she interrupted, "but seriously, I'm . . . Ouch! I'm fine. And for the record I'm not waiting on Ben, and I'm not single." Marilyn touched her ear and examined her hand. She was surprised not to see blood. She thanked Nikki and promised to call her later.

"Sorry, Mommy," Bianca apologized after seeing Marilyn jump. She wanted her mommy to have a French roll like her teacher, Miss Morris. Not wanting to feel left out, B.J. was busy polishing his mother's toes. He promised her that they were going to be prettier than Chee Chee, their neighbor's poodle.

Marilyn knew Nikki was concerned about her. With Reggie *incarcerated and also having to raise twins* she did have her hands full. She was thankful to have a friend like Nikki *who always offered to baby sit while she went to shop or ran errands.* One who always offered to baby-sit while she went shopping or got her nails done. Marilyn had always been low maintenance or as Nikki liked to say "no maintenance." Her husband and her son were all she had needed to be happy. She was now learning to find fulfillment in her job and her children.

Marilyn smiled as Bianca patted her hair. If there was one thing she wasn't feeling these days, it was loneliness. She flinched as the wet polish dripped between her toes.

The doorbell buzzed.

"Wait just a minute," she said, as she stuffed cotton balls between her toes. On her heels she hobbled across the floor. She looked out the window. It was Aunt Liz.

"Aunt Liz, this is a pleasant surprise" she exclaimed.

"I see you've changed beauticians," Aunt Liz snickered, as she closed the door.

Marilyn caught her reflection in the mirror and proudly patted her lopsided French roll. She pushed down several hairpins that were sticking up. *As Marilyn hobbled across the room, Aunt Liz looked down at her niece's feet and added* "You finally decided to get a pedicure. Well, it's about time. What did you do, come into an inheritance? Sorry. But seriously, I just came by to ask about Reggie. Does he seem okay? Is he eating? When can Robert and I go see him?"

Marilyn tried to answer all of her questions. "Yes, he seems okay. He has lost a little weight, but he says the food isn't any worst than school. You and Uncle Robert can visit anytime. He added your names to the list."

Marilyn thanked her for keeping the twins for the weekend. Aunt Liz assured her that the pleasure was theirs.

"I truly enjoyed my great-niece and nephew this weekend. I don't know when I've had so much fun. We have never had three children in the house at the same time."

Marilyn looked puzzled.

"Bianca, B.J. and your Uncle Robert," she joked.

Aunt Liz tried to hold a straight face as Marilyn looked down at her hands and feet. Her fingernails and cuticles were covered with bright red polish. There was polish on her knuckles as well. Aunt Liz quickly covered her mouth with her hand *but her eyes had already spoken.* Her eyes betrayed her.

Marilyn smiled mischievously, "I'm sure Bianca will be glad to do your hair today, Aunt Liz. Won't you sweetheart?"

"I'll do your toes, Auntie Liz!" B.J. cried enthusiastically.

Aunt Liz's mouth dropped. She stuttered "That's . . . that's awfully sweet of you kids but, but first you have to finish your mom's."

"Oh no, they can do mine's any ole time," she shot back, not letting her off the hook that easily. Aunt Liz rolled her eyes at Marilyn. Marilyn smiled victoriously.

Aunt Liz's face lit up as she remembered why she stopped by. "I have to run to the store and wanted to see if I could get someone to ride with me. I'm buying ice cream." }

"I will," they sang *and jumped* up and down. *They turned to Marilyn and pleaded "can we mom?"*

"You can go; wash your face and hands," Marilyn as they ran out of the door.

"Whew, that was close," confessed Aunt Liz, *while* holding her chest. "For a moment I thought I was going to be looking like you," she added.

They broke into a hearty laugh. Marilyn stopped long enough to warn her, "Be careful of making fun of guinea pigs. You may just end up being one."

Chapter Sixteen

After checking into the hotel Ben took a cab to the hospital. He didn't bother to unpack. The closer he got to the hospital, *the tighter the knot in his stomach became.* It never failed. Visiting them always caused him to hyperventilate. An acidic taste made it's way up his throat as he wiped his sweaty palms down the sides of his pants.

The nurse's station was empty. The only sounds came from the rooms as he passed the open doors.

Two-zero-nine.

Two-eleven.

Two-thirteen.

He stared down one side of the hall and stopped in front of two-fifteen. A soft laughter caught his attention as he slowly pushed open the door. Across the hall a young lady was sitting on the bed talking to an elderly woman. From the young lady's wrist hung a silver charm bracelet. He couldn't make out the charms but it immediately reminded him of an incident with Reggie years earlier.

One of Marilyn's co-workers had given Reggie a bank for his third birthday. It was a tall clown *which stood* over three feet tall. Each weekend Ben and Marilyn would dump in their loose coins. They wanted to fill it by the time Reggie started school.

As promised, Ben allowed Reggie to break it on his sixth birthday. He would be able to keep a hundred dollars for presents and the rest would be put into a savings account.

Reggie was so excited the night before his birthday, as they counted his money. By his calculations he had over a million, trillion dollars. Ben counted *$311.23*. Reggie was the happiest child in the neighborhood.

He excitedly shared with everyone that would listen that it was his birthday. Before shopping, they took him to the bank to open a savings account in his name. He whined until Marilyn allowed him to carry his passbook and his birthday money.

They entered the mall and headed straight to the toy store. *As they passed . . . Ben reminded Reggie* that his birthday was two days before Aunt Liz's *and pointed to a charm bracelet.* He suggested that Reggie buy it for her. Ben assured Reggie that it would make Aunt Liz very happy. Reggie stared at the floor.

Marilyn pulled a twenty from Reggie's hand *and* reassured Reggie that he would have enough to get his gifts. Reggie wasn't convinced.

He snatched the twenty from Marilyn.

Reggie stated, "Daddy said this was all my money. Didn't you, Daddy?"

"Yes, I did Reggie. It is your money. Don't you want to make Aunt Liz happy for her birthday?"

"I'm going to buy me a lot of toys!"—*and started naming one toy after another.*

Marilyn tried again. "Reggie look" *as she pointed at the bracelet.* "There a place to put a picture. Whose picture do you think she'd put in there?"

"Mines!" Reggie announced joyfully.

"Right!" Marilyn agreed, taking a twenty out of his hand.

"It only cost one of these. You still have one, two, three, four," she encouraged.

Reggie's countenance fell.

Ben asked again, "Don't you want Aunt Liz to be happy?"

"Yes, but she's not a little kid," he shot back.

"No, she's not a kid. But just as you like getting gifts, so do older people." Ben replied, annoyed with Reggie's selfishness.

Seeing that they were getting no where, Ben tried a tougher approach. "Well Marilyn, there's only one thing to do. We have to give Aunt Liz her gift back. It wouldn't be fair for Reggie to keep her gift if he's not willing to make her happy by buying her something special."

Reggie's eyes darted from the money to the bracelet and back again. *He was clearly thinking about the big* box in the hall closet Uncle Robert had brought over that morning.

"Okay," he said, *as he reluctantly gave Ben one of the bills.*

*   *   *

"Sir. Excuse me, please." A custodian pointed to a spill on the floor. "Sorry," Ben replied, stepping over what looked like spilled milk. *The jingle startled Ben out of his reverie. He looked up to see a young girl closing the door and realized he had been staring at her bracelet. Ben pushed* opened the door, the room was dark although the shades were opened. Rain was in the forecast. A soft humming came from the machine at the head of the bed. Ben stood in the doorway.

Mr. Saunders was Ben's father's closest friend since high school. They had worked together for years. Mr. Saunders had often gone fishing and to baseball games with Ben and his dad. After Ben graduated from high school, Mr. Saunders married and moved to

Ohio. He, however, came home several times a year to visit family and friends.

"Ben is that you?" he asked, as he strained to see.

"Yes, sir," Ben replied as he slowly walked to the foot of the bed. He gently patted Mr. Saunders' foot. He motioned for Ben to come closer. Ben *hesitated.*

Mr. Saunders clutched the bed rails and slowly shifted his weight backward.

"Your dad came to visit the other day. I see you got my message," he reached for Ben's hand. *He broke into quick bursts of coughs and withdrew his hand.* Quickly he withdrew his hand as he broke into a series of coughs. Yellowish green mucus ran down the side of his mouth as he struggled to catch his breath. With his eyes closed he felt for the box of tissues. *Ben pulled out a couple of tissues and placed them in his hand.* Mr. Saunders looked much older than Ben remembered. His body, once strong and robust, was now frail. What was left of his full head of wavy black hair was now white. It was thin and strategically combed to the front, unsuccessfully hiding a deep receding hairline.

Ben's heart went out to him as he watched the mucus slide down *Mr. Saunder's* chin and onto his gown. Ben took a tissue and wiped his face and the gown. He threw the tissues in the wastebasket.

"Ben. Did you hear the news? Did they tell you?" he asked excitedly.

Ben nodded "Yes, mom told me."

"All of these years I thought that God didn't love me. I thought I had messed up too bad." He shook his head "I did some foolish things when I was younger, and made a lot of mistakes. I thought I wasn't good enough to go to church, so I didn't."

He sat up straight. "You know what? This nurse came in two weeks ago, and she told me that God loves me. Me! Can you believe it? She said God wants me to live with Him forever."

He started coughing and reached for his cup of water. Gently, Ben held it to his mouth. He took a sip and motioned that he'd had enough.

"Ben, I couldn't get on my knees but that night I laid in bed and I told God I was sorry. I told Him I wish I could make it right. But, I can't. Some of the people are dead. Some have moved."

Fighting back tears he continued, "I left my first wife after twelve years."

Ben looked surprised, "I didn't know you were . . ."

"Only a few people knew I was married before. Your parents did."

He turned his head to the wall. "We were always arguing about Little John. She didn't believe in spanking at all." He was silent. Ben looked to see whether he had fallen asleep.

"I'm okay. Just a little tired."

"Your Dad told me about you and May Lynn." Ben smiled at the way he pronounced Marilyn's name.

"Son"—he always called Ben son when he was about to give him fatherly advice.

"Don't walk away from your responsibilities like I did, no matter how tough things become. I learned later that my son started hanging out with the wrong crowd. His mom hated being the bad guy so she let him have his way. He was getting in trouble at school, and his mom thought the teachers were singling him out; she was in denial. By the time she woke up he was fifteen and wouldn't listen to a thing she said."

Ben wondered if Mr. Saunders' son knew he was in the hospital. Maybe he could find him before it was too late.

"Where does your son live?" Ben asked. Mr. Saunders shook his head and turned to the wall. Ben could tell he was crying.

"One day he and two of his friends *were playing hooky from school and riding in his friend's car.* The streets were icy.

The witnesses said they were driving too fast for the conditions. They hit a tree and Little John didn't make it. I was so distraught, I stopped taking my medicine. My immune system was weak, and a couple of weeks ago I was on my way out. But after the nurse prayed for me and I talked to God . . . ."

Clearing his throat, he said, "I still have this hacking cough but the doctor said I might go home next week."

He beckoned for Ben to come closer. Getting up, Ben pulled the chair closer to the bed.

Mr. Saunders reached for Ben's hand. "Son, don't make the same mistake that I made with my wife and son. Call me henpecked. I let them both down. I was always trying to keep peace, but look at the price I paid."

Shaking his head, *he added* "You know what's the funny thing? I still didn't have peace. What I learned is too late for me, but it's not for you. I know you and May Lynn have something special. You have something only a few find in a lifetime. Don't throw it away," he pleaded.

Choking back tears he ordered Ben, "Go on, and get out of here. Find your wife. Your marriage is worth fighting for. Besides your sons and daughter need you."

Ben's mouth dropped.

"Sons?"

"Daughter?"

Mr. Saunders nodded, "Twins. They are five, no six, I believe. The boy looks just like you. He's a handsome little fellow. The girl is a beauty, just like her mom."

"You mean . . . ."

Mr. Saunders was feeling tired but he had to explain. He couldn't leave him with a lot of unanswered questions.

"Marilyn found out about a month after you left that she was pregnant. She didn't want you to come back out of guilt. We all begged her to tell you, but she refused. She even threatened to move out of town if we told you, and we knew she wasn't making an idle threat. Please, don't be mad at us. We had no choice."

"It wasn't your fault. I'm the one responsible." Ben walked *over to the window, turned the handle, and opened it.* A cool breeze rushed in.

"I love this time of the year," announced Mr. Saunders, breathing deeply.

"Excuse me. I guess I had too much coffee. I have to find the washroom," said Ben, walking toward the door.

"It's right behind you. As the old folk uses to say, if it had been a snake it would have *bitten* you," he teased.

"Hospitals don't like the visitors to use the patient's washroom," Ben reminded him.

"Look, I've been here two weeks and I've never even looked inside. Besides, I'll have a lot of explaining to do if my nurse walks in and see a puddle on the floor."

He chuckled and pulled the blanket.

"Since you put it that way," Ben rushed in and closed the door.

Mr. Saunders hadn't seen Ben in six years. He couldn't help marveling at how much he looked like his father.

He even walked like him.

"Knock!"

"Knock!"

"You locked yourself in?" Mr. Saunders asked with his face to the wall.

"Are you asleep?" Marilyn asked, as she opened the door.

"No, just relaxing," Mr. Saunders *answered*. He turned over expecting to see his nurse.

"Well, well. If it isn't the one person I was just thinking about."

She walked to the bed and gave him a big hug.

"I can't believe you are here! Two of my favorite people here at the same time."

Hearing the running water Marilyn asked "Who's your visitor?" *She hung her purse on the back of the chair and pulled it closer to the bed.*

"He's going to be surprised!"

"Who? Who is going to be surprised?"

"Benjamin! He's in there!" he shouted excited.

Without a word Marilyn grabbed her purse. "I'm sorry."

"I'll be back," she called over her shoulder as she headed for the door.

As she hurried past the nurse's station, she dropped her purse. One of the doctors looked up from his chart. Seeing her expression, he rushed to Mr. Saunders' room. Marilyn picked up her purse and hurried down the corridor.

She waited anxiously for the DOWN elevator. All kinds of emotions began to well up inside. A part of her wanted to cry. A part was happy he was okay. She wanted to go back and confront him. She wanted to get as far away as possible.

The bell chimed.

It was going up.

As she paced back and forth she knew she had to keep moving. If she stood still, she might break down. *She noticed the exit sign and headed* for the stairs. She had to get to the outside. She needed fresh air.

Reaching the first floor, she hurled the door open. *It hit an intern and knocked and knocked* a stack of papers out of his hands. Hundreds of sheets of paper scattered over the corridor floor. *The intern was livid and shouted unprofessional words."*

"Sorry!" Marilyn shouted over her shoulder, *without breaking stride.*

"Sorry is not going to get these papers back in order!" he *bellowed.*

Looking around in disbelief he shook his head. Slowly, he dropped down on his knees and began to pick up the papers and carefully turned them in the same direction.

The elevator door opened and two elderly gentlemen wearing lab coats stepped out. They saw the intern crawling around the floor picking up papers and stopped to help.

"Thanks," he said as they handed him the last sheets.

Seeing their expressions, he begged, "Please, don't ask."

They smiled and walked off.

As he pushed the UP button, he turned and called out "I just want you to know that one of your patients may be missing." He pointed down the corridor as Marilyn passed the front desk.

"Thanks for the info," Dr. James responded *tipped* his head with a folder. He was the chief of the psychiatric ward.

Chapter Seventeen

Marilyn's heart rejoiced as she listened to the twins *sing* along with Dora. They knew Mommy wasn't feeling well. *They had fixed peanut butter and jelly sandwiches. Afterwards, they sprawled across the living room floor in their pajamas and quietly watched cartoons.* She had given them their bath early.

Marilyn was getting a summer cold. It had to be from the car's air conditioner on the trip to visit Reggie. She poured herself a spoonful of medicine. *She stood over the sink and stared at the spoon.* She hated taking medicine. But the cold had *sapp*ed her of her energy. This was the one medicine her father took for a cold—castor oil. She was desperate for some relief.

Marilyn picked up the glass she had used earlier. After rinsing it out, she filled it with tap water. She held the spoon in one hand and the water in the other. At the same time she brought her hands to her mouth. She quickly drank the medicine and washed it down with the glass of water.

"Yuck!" she *sighed and shook her head. She screwed the cap back on the bottle and placed* the bottle on the top cabinet shelf. She pushed it out of the twins' view.

Her attention was drawn to a photo magnet of Reggie, Ben and herself. It was taken in the mall a month before Ben left. Yesterday, at the hospital she was unsure of what she wanted. Now that she had time to think, she was hoping he would call. She wanted to tell him about Reggie and about the twins.

The doorbell rang.

It was probably Nikki. She was the only one who felt close enough to just drop in unexpectedly. Marilyn pulled back the drapery.

"Ah!" she gasped. Covering her mouth she slumped down in the chair.

The twins rushed to her side.

"Don't cry, Mommy. It's going to be all right," said Bianca as she brushed her mom's hair from her face.

She left traces of peanut butter and jelly along her hairline

The doorbell rang again followed by a knock.

"Mommy, somebody's at our door!" B.J. cried.

Wiping her face with the back of her hand, she rose to her feet. Slowly she walked over to the door. The twins followed close behind.

Sniffing, Marilyn turned to them, "I need you to do me a big favor. I need you to go to your room and play. I'll call you okay?" She kneeled down and gave both of them a kiss. *B.J. wiped his kiss off.*

"Okay," they sang in unison *and raced* to their room. *With her hand on the door, she took a deep breath, wiped the peanut butter off the side of her face and opened the door.*

"Hi Marilyn, how are you doing?" Dumb. Dumb. Dumb. It wasn't what he wanted to say. But how do you greet your wife after being gone six years?

"Hi Ben," she said without showing any emotions.

"May I please come in?" He asked, while holding his breath.

He certainly wouldn't blame her if she said no. Without answering, Marilyn stepped back and motioned for him to come in. Closing the door, she followed him into the living room.

Ben began to sweat. Rolling up his shirt sleeves, he sat on the couch.

He moved over making room for Marilyn. She sat in the chair across from him. The twins were watching from down the hall. She made eye contact with them, and they went into their room.

"You . . . you look well." Dumb. Dumb. Dumb. That's like saying, considering you've had to raise three kids by yourself. "Lord, help me. Don't let me mess this up," Ben prayed. He could feel beads of perspiration on his brow.

"Thanks, so do you," she replied. With a twenty-pound weight loss that he couldn't afford to lose and dark circles under his eyes because of a lack of sleep, he knew she was being kind.

"Mom told me the latest about Reggie. How is he? Can I go see him?" he asked. He wasn't even sure Reggie would want to see him.

"Yes, he just has to put your name on the visitor's list."

"Marilyn, what happened? What exactly did he do?" He felt somehow responsible. Things may have turned out differently if he had been home.

"He stole a credit card from his teacher's briefcase and forged his signature, making several expensive purchases.

"What was he buying?"

"Some kind of boots all the kids are wearing. They are called Forest land or Tree land, or something. The name has to do with tree or wood. He had asked me to get him a pair. I promised him I would on two conditions: he had to stay out of trouble and do well in school. He didn't fulfill his part of the bargain, so neither did I."

The door was closed to the bedroom, but she could hear the twins arguing. They were getting louder.

"Excuse me, please," Marilyn said, getting up. The twins came running down the hall.

"Yes, he is!" exclaimed Bianca.

"No. He's not! I'm gonna ask him!" cried B.J. Bianca followed him into the living room carrying a photograph.

B.J. walked boldly up to Ben and asked, "Are you our daddy?"

Ben was caught off guard. Helplessly he looked to Marilyn for a clue. Is this the way she wanted to tell them? Marilyn stared at the floor. Realizing he was on his own. He stood up. It was getting warm in the room.

"Yes, I'm your father."

"See. I told you," said Bianca waving the picture in B.J.'s face.

"Why don't you live with us?" B.J. asked.

"Because he don't love us," Bianca said sadly.

How could he make a six year old understand when he didn't understand fully, himself.

"That's you, Grandpa . . . ," said Bianca pointing at the photo. Marilyn couldn't hold back the tears. She started to cry softly.

"You made Mommy cry," accused B.J., as he and his sister rushed to Marilyn's side.

"Don't cry Mommy."

"Mommy's fine. Now get ready for bed. It's getting late. I'll be there to tuck you in," said Marilyn.

They gave her a hug and raced to their room. Bianca stopped suddenly. She pointed her little finger. "You better not make Mommy cry."

"I promise. I never want to make Mommy cry again."

He cleared his throat. "Marilyn, I want . . . ."

She raised her hand. "Listen," she whispered. Together they listened while the twins prayed. Bianca's voice was soft. They couldn't understand what she was saying but B.J.'s requests were very clear.

"God, this is B.J. God bless Mommy, God bless Reggie. God bless Uncle Robert. God bless Aunt Liz. God bless Grandma. God bless Grandpa. Amen. Oh, I forgot God bless daddy and let him stay with us. Amen. Oh, yeah bless Bianca, Amen."

Ben got up from the couch and walked over to her chair. He kneeled down on one knee. He took her hands. He was so full with emotion from hearing his son pray he could hardly speak.

"Marilyn, I want to come home if you will have me back."

She sat weeping and fidgeting with the buttons on her blouse.

He pleaded, "Give me another chance. I was wrong to walk away . . . from you . . . from my family. I've been miserable without you. I tried burying myself in my work. I worked ten and twelve hours a day. Still, at night I found it hard to sleep. I know it's going to take time. But I want our relationship to be like it was before."

"Our relationship can never be like it was Ben," she said pushing up from the chair. "You see, I'm not the same person. Things have changed," she said *and walked* over to the window.

Every ounce of hope in him faded. "I'm not surprised. I guess I was hoping that maybe . . . . it was plain silly for me to think that after six years . . . . any man would be glad to have you in his life."

He got off his knees and continued continued, "I guess I'll be going. I'll come by tomorrow morning to see the kids if it's okay with you." With his head down he headed toward the door. He had to get out before he started sobbing like a baby.

"We won't be home until after one. The twins and I are going to church tomorrow with Aunt Liz and Uncle Robert. You see, I've given my life to the Lord. It happened yesterday after I ran out of the hospital. I was sitting in my car soaking wet having a pity party," she said throwing her hands up. "When I looked and saw a paper stuck on my windshield wiper. I cut the wipers on but it wouldn't move. So, I got out and crumbled it up. I didn't want to litter so I put it on the floor of the car."

"Later when I got home I was about to throw it in the garbage when I saw in big bold print: S-A-L. Always looking for a sale, I opened the crumbled paper to check it out." She stopped. "It was better than a sale's ad it was about SALVATION.

"Wait right here," she ran down the hall.

"Here it is," she said from the back room. Proudly, holding it up as a trophy she walked back into the living room. He had the biggest grin, on his face that she had ever seen.

"What?" she asked puzzled.

"I didn't think there were words that would sound sweeter than the two you said on our wedding day, but the ones you just said, *I've accepted Jesus as my Lord and Savior.*"

Pointing up toward heaven *he went on,* "I guess He has been dealing with both of us. You won't believe this, but, I've accepted Him, too."

She rushed into his arms. Ben choked back tears. "I'm so sorry for all the pain I've caused you. I don't feel that I had a right to even ask to come back after being gone for six years. The truth is I can't see myself another day without you."

He gently tilted her face upward and said, "Please, I want to come home."

"I want to be here for the twins and to help Reggie when he comes home. This time I want to be a real father not just the bread winner," he said looking in her eyes.

She understood what he was saying. *She pulled his hand down and turned away.* Confused, she sat on the end of the couch. She had mixed feelings. A part of her wanted that more than anything, yet, another part was afraid her heart would be broken, again. Would they be happy? Would he leave again?

"I know what you are feeling. You're wondering how long will it be before I get tired and leave again." He vowed, "Never, I promise, never again."

She searched his face wanting desperately to believe his promise.

"What make you think this time will be different?" she asked.

Pointing *upward,* he smiled. "Now we have help."

Epilogue

Marilyn and Ben talked for hours after tucking the twins into bed. She promised to call the facility as soon as possible to have Reggie add Ben's name to the visitor's list. He promised to call T.J. first thing in the morning and ask him to ship a few things and give the rest to a charity He wouldn't be returning to California.

"Do you mind if I catch the end of the news?" he asked, noticing the time. It was *10:20.*

"No," replied Marilyn, *while passing* him the remote control.

He started flipping through the channels.

"Stop!" cried Marilyn sitting up straight. On the screen was a young, newly married couple being interviewed.

He was explaining that he was the youth pastor at his church, and God had given him a message on parenting. The title caught Marilyn's attention:

MISTAKES PARENTS MADE IN THE BIBLE.

"Let's watch this please?" Marilyn asked. Ben nodded.

The youth pastor began to explain how God had taught him about parenting before he met his wife. During his first year in ministry, the senior pastor had asked him to speak on Father's Day.

The youth pastor said, "I had never spoken before a large crowd; needless to say, I was terrified. So I did the only thing I knew to do.

I fell on my face and prayed. God is faithful. He showed me in the book of Proverbs, principles for parenting. He also gave me three examples of His people not following those principles. First, He took me to Genesis 27:10, where He showed me how Jacob's mother, Rebekah, conspired to help her favorite son get the father's blessing. Secondly He took me to 1 Samuel 3:13, where He showed me how Eli, a priest, failed to restrain his sons, which resulted in their death. Thirdly, He showed me how Samson's parent helped him to marry a Philistine woman, even though the Mosaic Law forbade it, and how eventually it was a Philistine woman who brought him to his death in Judges 14."

Ben looked at Marilyn. They knew God was ministering to them. She reached for his hand.

About the Author

Catharine has been married to Thomas Ingram for thirty nine years. They have three children; Michael, Michelle and Derandel.

Catharine Ingram was born in Shaw, a small rural town in the Mississippi Delta. She has always enjoyed reading and writing short stories.